On Your Own

On Your Own

A College Readiness Guide
for Teens With ADHD/LD

Patricia O. Quinn, MD

and Theresa E. Laurie Maitland, PhD

Magination Press • Washington, DC

American Psychological Association

Published by

MAGINATION PRESS
An Educational Publishing Foundation Book
American Psychological Association
750 First Street, NE
Washington, DC 20002

For more information about our books, including a complete catalog, please write to us, call 1-800-374-2721, or visit our website at www.apa.org/pubs/magination.

Book and cover design by Bryan Ische
Printed by Worzalla, Stevens Points, Wisconsin

Library of Congress Cataloging-in-Publication Data
Quinn, Patricia O.
  On your own: a college readiness guide for teens with ADHD/LD / Patricia O. Quinn and Theresa E. Laurie Maitland.
    p. cm.
  "American Psychological Association."
  Includes bibliographical references.
  ISBN-13: 978-1-4338-0955-2 (pbk.)
  ISBN-10: 1-4338-0955-9 (pbk.)
  1. Learning disabled youth--Education (Higher)--United States. 2. Learning disabled youth--Education (Secondary)--United States. 3. College student orientation--United States. I. Maitland, Theresa L., 1947- II. American Psycological Association. III. Title.
  LC4704.5 Q85 2011
  371.94--dc22
                2011007779

10 9 8 7 6 5 4 3 2 1

Contents

Part I: Get Ready   7

COLLEGE IS **NOT** HIGH SCHOOL   11

No Homework and Not Much Structure   11
No Parents   12
No Accommodations   15
No Teachers   16
Thinking About These Differences   17

HOW TO USE THIS GUIDE   19

Step One: Complete the College Readiness Checklist   21
Step Two: Complete the Skills Analysis Worksheet   27
Step Three: Write Specific Goal Statements   28
Step Four: Create an Action Plan   33
Step Five: Develop a System to Track Your Progress   35
Step Six: Evaluate and Modify Your Plan   35

Part II: Get Set

36

SELF-DETERMINATION SKILLS

39

Self-Knowledge 39
Self-Advocacy and Communication Skills 47
Self-Management 55

DAILY LIVING SKILLS

65

Self-Care 66
Organization 79
Time Management 83

ACADEMIC SKILLS

93

Self-Knowledge 93
Study Skills 97
Time Management 112

Part III: Go!

121

Preparing to Start College 122
A Few Final Words 126
References 127

Part I: Get Ready

A re you dreaming of the day when you go off to college? There's so much to look forward to. However, many teens diagnosed with Attention-Deficit Hyperactivity Disorder (ADHD) or learning disabilities, disorders, or differences (LD) worry that college might be too difficult for them. We are here to tell you that's simply not the case. Many students with ADHD/LD graduate from college every year. In fact, many more students with these differences are now attending college and many of these colleges have programs set up to help them once they get on campus. Also, with all the technology available to everyone, now may be a perfect time to be a teen with ADHD/LD. College isn't easy, but if you are informed and prepared before you get there and know how to get the help you need, you'll have an excellent chance for succeeding and reaching your ultimate goal—graduation!

You're probably already thinking about the adjustments that college will require. It's good to think about these changes, because successfully adjusting to college is a real accomplishment that can be more challenging than most teens ever imagine. Not all teens who attend college succeed once they're there. According to studies conducted by the National Center for Education Statistics, only 6 out of 10 students who start college are still enrolled or have graduated 5–6 years later—and these are students without diagnosed disabilities. These same studies suggest that students with disabilities may graduate or stay in college at an even lower rate, reporting that only 50%

of students with disabilities who start college may still be there or have graduated 5–6 years later.[1]

Studies also indicate that college students may be experiencing more emotional and mental health problems than in the past, thanks to all the pressures young people feel about their futures and trying to figure out who they are.[2] Not many studies have been done to look specifically at the graduation rates of students with ADHD/LD, but those that have been done suggest that students with these difficulties may graduate at an even lower rate and may have an even tougher time successfully adjusting to life on their own at college and the more difficult academic expectations they meet there.[3]

The good news is that as a teen with ADHD/LD, you've probably already faced and overcome many challenges and made adjustments throughout your life. You already have a toolbox full of what it takes to be successful. First, you know that you have ADHD/LD and that you want to go to college—otherwise you wouldn't be reading this guide. You already have lots of experience dealing with difficulties caused by these differences and you already know that while they can sometimes make things more difficult for you, they can also help you see things differently than other people. Maybe you even see gifts hidden in all the challenges you have faced. You have most likely learned that with hard work and some additional supports, you have been and can be successful.

College will require that you add some new tools to the ones you already have. Even the best prepared teens, who have attended

· · · · · · · · · · · · · · · · · · ·

1   National Center for Education Statistics (2000, 2002).

2   Kadison and DiGeronimo (2004); Sieben (2011).

3   Some studies that address the college experiences of students with ADHD/ LD include: Barkley, Murphy, and Fischer (2007); D'Amico (personal communication, January 29, 2008); Heiligenstein, Guenther, Levey, Savino, and Fulwiler (1999); Klein (2011); Murray, Goldstein, Nourse, and Edgar (2000); Newman, Wagner, Cameto, and Knokey (2009); Rabiner, Anastopoulos, Costello, Hoyle, and Swartzwelder (2008); Vogel and Adelman (1990a, 1990b, 1991, 2000); Vogel, Leonard, Scales, Hayeslip, Hermansen, and Donnells (1998); and Wagner, Newman, Cameto, Garza, and Levine (2005).

the toughest academic high schools and who have had the strongest ADHD/LD support, need to know that they'll very likely face many expected, and unexpected, challenges and adjustments in college. After only a few weeks at college, one teen summed it up this way: "Being in college is like being a kid in a candy store without the owner, and even though I hated how my parents nagged me, now I realize I don't know how to nag myself." There is a lot you can do to use the time in high school to get ready for the reality of life on your own at college. This guide will help you stretch and grow while you're still in high school by giving you more information about what you will face in college and helping you create a personalized college readiness plan for how to improve the skills you already have and develop the new skills you will need once you are there.

College Is
Not High School

O k, you already knew that. However, anticipating the differences between high school and college will not only help
you prepare for the challenges, but it will allow you to look
forward to some truly awesome new freedoms. Let's begin by looking at
some of the ways that college is different (and better!) than high school,
and the freedoms and challenges you're likely to encounter there.

NO HOMEWORK AND
NOT MUCH STRUCTURE

Maybe we're exaggerating, but homework in college might be totally
unrecognizable compared to the nightly assignments you're probably
used to in high school. And you will have the opportunity to decide how
to structure your life on your own.

If you've hated high school with its predictable daily schedule and consistent work patterns
and rigid class requirements, you might be
looking forward to not having the same daily
schedule or graded homework every night.
At college you won't have the same classes and

schedule every day, all day, and some of your classes may meet in the evenings. Some days you may not even have any classes. Sleeping late on the days you don't have classes and heading to a coffee shop to study with friends sounds great . . . but!

Students with ADHD/LD often struggle with time management and have poor *executive functioning skills*—the skills needed to make a plan or set a goal and stick to it until that goal is completed. For you and many students with ADHD/LD, managing time and completing tasks on your own can be really difficult. Without the structure of daily graded homework or weekly tests keeping the pressure on, assignments can get put off until the last minute or may not get done at all. Now is the time to learn how to stay on top of things and use your free time to get things done before a big deadline hits.

Without a structured and balanced weekly schedule, it's easy for any student, even ones without ADHD/LD, to fall into patterns of all-or-nothing living—relaxing when nothing is due and pulling all-nighters to cram for tests or finish papers and projects at exam time. Some students can squeak by in this all-or-nothing mode, but if you have difficulties learning or struggle with those important executive functioning skills, you might not be as successful as your classmates at completing all the readings or functioning without sleep when it is time to get in gear with academics. You may feel the stress of difficult times even more than your friends, too. Now is a great time for you to prepare for these challenges so that you can enjoy your college experience without having to stress out too much during the crunch times.

NO PARENTS

No curfews. No one telling you to study or clean your room. No one checking on your homework. No one telling you when to eat or how you can spend your money. You finally get to be your own boss! That may sound especially good to you depending on how much involvement your parents have had in your life up to this point.

PARENT WARRIORS, PARENT DIRECTORS, AND PARENT REPAIRMEN

When their children are diagnosed with ADHD/LD, we often find parents react by trying to protect their children and make up for those executive functioning problems we talked about before. Their responses tend to fall into one of several common roles: the Parent Warriors, the Parent Repairmen, and the Parent Fixers.

PARENT WARRIORS

Parent warriors have been on a mission to fight for their child with ADHD/LD since the diagnosis was made. They participate in every battle that needs to be fought to ensure that their child is understood, treated fairly, and given all the services necessary for success.

Without parent warriors, many teens would never even be able to dream of attending college, but the downside of this parenting pattern is that you may have missed out on the opportunity to handle the challenges that will be part of life after high school. It's important to remember that warrior parents are just trying to protect you, but now is a great time to learn how to protect yourself—and that might mean helping your parents to put down those swords.

PARENT DIRECTORS

Parent directors are naturals at noticing small problems, reading warning signs, taking charge, and problem-solving. If you have a parent director, they may have fallen into a pattern of telling you how to get a difficult project done, clean your room, or handle a conflict with a friend. They might even quickly pitch in to help. High school is the perfect time to start working with them on identifying what they have been doing, developing your own problem-solving skills, and learning how you can direct yourself.

PARENT REPAIRMEN

Maybe instead of fighting your battles or warding off problems, your parents act more like repairmen—fixing problems
that happen as a result of your attention and self-management
challenges. For example, rather than fighting for test-taking
accommodations, they fix things like low grades after the fact
by talking to teachers and arranging re-takes. Or, instead of
checking on progress and directing projects, they call a teacher
when it's clear the project or paper won't get done and arrange an
extension. Now's a good time to think about what could happen
in college if you don't have someone around to make things go
smoothly or fix problems once things have gone wrong. You can
start working on the skills you need to put the repairmen out of
business before you even go away to school.

Knowing about these roles can be useful for figuring out how to
talk to your parents about the steps you're taking to adjust from
high school to college. You'll see boxes throughout this book that
provide more ideas.

Even though they still love and care about you, your
parents probably won't be there for you the way
they were in high school. With no one to wake
you up in the morning or to drive you to school if
you oversleep and miss your ride, you get to figure
out how to do it all! What problems do you imagine
might arise if your parents are no longer readily available to fight for
you, direct you, prevent any problems, or bail you out? Now is the
time to identify what role your parents are playing in your life and
start taking over some of those tasks for yourself.

NO ACCOMMODATIONS

Again, no accommodations is an exaggeration—there are certainly a lot of things you are allowed to ask for at college, but the rules for managing your ADHD/LD might look a bit different.

At college, no one will know about your disabilities if you don't tell them and no one can force you to go to tutors or therapists or special education classes. That isn't how things work at college and no one—not even your parents—can make you get help or take your medications.

It can be tempting to start out at college with a clean slate—without all the fuss of ADHD/LD. Over the years, we've watched some teens go off to college and try to leave their learning differences in high school. One teen even told us that before college he really thought his mother and the doctor he saw made too much of a fuss about his ADHD/LD and that he "didn't think they were real," only to find out that he couldn't hide from his differences for very long and be successful. High school may be the perfect time to get a better understanding of how your disability affects you in learning and in life. Deciding what accommodations and services are essential for avoiding a struggle at college and learning how to seek out and ask for help so that you can do as well as you would like may be the keys to your success.

To start, you'll need to find out if the accommodations you've received in high school will be there in college. Do the same laws exist at the college level? Can you still get reduced workloads, extensions for reports and assignments, exemptions for poor spelling, and test modifications? Will you be exempt from taking math or foreign language classes? In college, professors are allowed to set their own course requirements and the disabilities offices can only mandate reasonable accommodations like extended time on tests, class notes, and audio books. Only an individual professor can decide to give a student an extension or an incomplete or change a written test to an oral exam. The college gets to decide which classes are required for all students to graduate, so all students may have to take math classes or foreign language classes—or at least try them with help before allowing a substitution or a waiver for these requirements.

Even if you know that all the help you are getting is important, you'll need to remember that in college it's up to you to be your own self-advocate and communicate your needs to others or there won't be any accommodations. Success in college is often highly dependent on the help you get for yourself.

NO TEACHERS

This one might sound a little weird, but it's sort of true. Instead of teachers, your classes will be led by professors or teaching assistants. The difference between teachers and professors is subtle, but important. Professors are doing much more than just teaching classes (some do research, publish papers, work at another job, or write books), and that has some serious implications for you as a student.

As we have already said, in college, many classes will not have daily homework or weekly quizzes. In fact, many classes only have a midterm and a final exam, or you might only have one big paper or project due at the end of the semester. Professors have office hours each week, when students can come and discuss class topics, and they don't see it as their job to nag and micromanage students and tell them what to do and when to do it. Being treated like this might sound great to you.

Professors are usually hired for their expertise in a certain subject, rather than for their teaching ability. They might present information quickly in large lecture classes and assign students lots of pages to read each week, expecting that college students know how to teach themselves. Profes-sors may not provide study guides or much detail on the course syllabi, and you'll have to learn for yourself how to determine what's important in lectures or reading assignments.

If you go to a smaller college or a community college, things might be more like what you are used to in high school and classes may have more teaching and more discussion. The classes for underclassmen at larger colleges and universities, though, may consist of a hundred or more students. There may be little opportunity for discussing subject matter or asking questions in class. That's why professors have office hours, but many new students find going to a college professor's office to be intimidating.

THINKING ABOUT THESE DIFFERENCES

Now is a good time to pause and think about your reactions to all of the differences and ideas that we've presented in the previous pages. First, try to define what you are feeling when you think about going to college. Are you anxious? Excited? Unsure? Prepared? Worried? It's normal if you are feeling a bit anxious and unsure. Talking about your feelings with your parents, a sister, brother, or friend may help you process these feelings and find solutions to problems. Your teachers or guidance counselor at school should also be knowledgeable about the differences between high school and college and may have worked with other students to ensure that they were ready to face successfully the many challenges at college. Remember that you've already been successful at adjusting to new expectations. Think about how you've handled changes in past and how you might want to handle them now.

Now is also a good time to get help for any more serious problems you may have with managing your emotions or with abusing drugs, alcohol, food, or even technology. These problems can get even bigger at college where you'll face more stress and more temptations with hardly any adult supervision. Some college campuses are notorious for having students who drink and party. If you have already experienced problems with substance abuse, a party school is probably the last place you should be. The many challenges you'll face as you adjust to life on your own at college can trigger any existing emotional problems. Just remember, there's help for all these issues in every community if you are willing to acknowledge your problems and to seek help.

With no homework, not much structure, no parents, no accommodations unless you arrange them, and no teachers, college is sure to be very different than what you are used to in high school. Learning about all these freedoms is a great reminder that you're ready to start practicing being on your own—being trusted to make decisions for yourself about your own life and getting things done your way, according to your values. But no one figures this stuff out overnight, and sometimes it's good to have a reality check and remind yourself that doing it all on your own can be both great and tough. While there are no guarantees in life, one thing is certain— college and life on your own are sure to be much easier if you are prepared.

How To Use This Guide

The purpose of this guide is to help you create a personalized college readiness plan to manage the transition that many students (even those who thought they were well-prepared) find difficult. The guide centers on the **College Readiness Checklist**, which contains a list of skills that we (and others) have found critical to students' success at college. Use the steps outlined below to develop your own personal readiness plan.

STEP ONE: Complete the College Readiness Checklist on page 21. This checklist is divided into three major skill sets: Self-Determination Skills, Daily Living Skills, and Academic Skills. Each of these sets contains questions about specific skills. By completing this checklist as honestly as possible, you'll get a good sense of the skills you'll need to work on during whatever time you have left in high school.

STEP TWO: Complete the Skills Analysis Worksheet. Decide on the one or two skills that you will work on each month (or week, if you have less time to prepare) during your years in high school. The Skills Analysis Worksheet on page 27 will help you decide how to structure this work.

STEP THREE: Write specific goal statements for each skill that you need to work on. Writing a specific goal statement can be difficult and may be a new concept for you or one of the skills that you need to develop. With practice, though, you'll be an expert at it before long.

The skill of writing goals is also included in the checklist under Self-Management Skills because we consider it to be important to success in college and life. You can rate yourself on it there.

STEP FOUR: Create an action plan to achieve your goals. Focus on how you plan to reach these goals during the coming weeks. To develop these plans, you can use the tips provided in Part II of this guide—they correspond to the skills you've already evaluated using the checklist, and we've provided lots of tips to get you started with each skill. We've also included **Books and Bookmarks**—a list of references for you to check out if you want to take your practice further.

STEP FIVE: Develop a system to track your progress.

STEP SIX: Evaluate and modify your plan.

Once you've reached your goal and mastered a skill, then choose another skill to work on. Continue this process in the time you have left in high until you feel better prepared to meet the challenges ahead.

This flow chart illustrates how the various steps work together to help you get ready by working on the skills you find you need to develop after completing the readiness checklist.

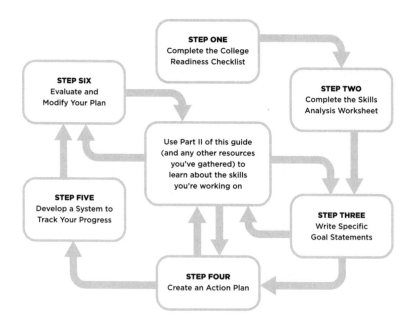

STEP ONE: COMPLETE THE COLLEGE READINESS CHECKLIST

Having read this far in this guide, you should now have a better understanding of how different things will be when you are on your own at college—what will be easy and present few obstacles for you and what could be more challenging. To check out where you stand on the path to college, it's time to rate yourself in the following areas to get a better idea of your strengths and weaknesses. There are no right or wrong answers—just your honest appraisal of how ready you are for taking charge as you move towards independent living. Be courageous and ask your parents, teachers, or friends to use this checklist and rate how prepared they think you are.

Rate each of the following items on a scale from 1 to 3, with 1 = not true of me, 2 = somewhat true of me, and 3 = very true of me. For any items rated 1 or 2, make a plan to improve in these areas before going to college. The numbers in parentheses refer to the pages in Part II where you will find information on each skill.

Self-Determination

I. SELF-KNOWLEDGE

I know a lot about myself and am aware of...

◯ my talents, interests, and my dreams for the future. (39)

◯ my feelings and reactions when I have to get used to new people, places, and situations and what helps me adjust. (42)

◯ my strengths and weaknesses in my academic and learning skills. (44)

YOUR SELF-KNOWLEDGE SCORE:

◯ /9 X 100 = ◯ %

II. SELF-ADVOCACY/COMMUNICATION SKILLS

I can...

◯ easily introduce myself to new people and hold conversations with others. (49)

◯ clearly express my strengths and weaknesses to my teachers or other people. (50)

◯ admit when I don't understand something in class and comfortably ask for help. (50)

◯ easily find the help or support I need when I have a problem. (51)

◯ express my thoughts well, even when I have a differing view or opinion, and stand firm when needed. (51)

◯ talk with the other people involved in any conflict and problem-solve to handle the situation. (53)

◯ participate in class discussions when this is expected of me. (54)

YOUR SELF-ADVOCACY/COMMUNICATION SCORE:

◯ /21 X 100 = ◯ %

III. SELF-MANAGEMENT

I can...

◯ regularly set realistic goals for myself in all areas of my life. (55)

◯ develop a plan to reach my goals and put it into action. (56)

◯ periodically think about my progress in reaching my goals and make modifications as needed. (56)

◯ persistently deal with any challenge, without becoming frustrated, until I find an acceptable solution. (57)

◯ observe my emotions, attention, and behavior and manage myself productively. (58)

◯ listen and understand what my family members are saying about me without getting defensive. (60)

◯ ask questions or ask to have the information repeated if I don't understand what someone is saying. (61)

YOUR SELF-MANAGEMENT SCORE:

◯ /21 X 100 = ◯ %

YOUR TOTAL SELF-DETERMINATION SCORE:

◯ /51 X 100 = ◯ %

Daily Living Skills

I. SELF-CARE

I can...

◯ wash and care for my own clothes. (66)

◯ take any medications I need with few or no reminders. (67)

◯ make my own appointments and call to refill my prescription medications. (69)

◯ prepare meals or choose healthy foods for my daily meals. (70)

◯ get adequate exercise to remain healthy. (73)

○ manage money well and be trusted with credit cards. (75)

○ make good decisions about how to handle stress. (77)

YOUR SELF-CARE SCORE:

○ /21 X 100 = ○ %

II. ORGANIZATION

I can...

○ organize my room and possessions with few
or no reminders. (79)

○ keep track of my important possessions and find them when
I need them. (82)

YOUR ORGANIZATION SCORE:

○ /6 X 100 = ○ %

III. TIME MANAGEMENT

I can...

○ get myself up and out the door each day. (83)

○ send myself to bed each night at a reasonable time. (85)

○ make good decisions about how to balance fun, chores, and
schoolwork. (88)

○ get places on time with no problem. (90)

YOUR TIME-MANAGEMENT SCORE:

◯ /12 X 100 = ◯ %

YOUR TOTAL DAILY LIVING SKILLS SCORE:

◯ /39 X 100 = ◯ %

Academic Skills

I. SELF-KNOWLEDGE

I know...

◯ my learning style and can find ways to help myself learn and study best in different classes. (93)

◯ when and where I need to study to get the best results. (95)

◯ how to motivate myself to face difficult assignments. (96)

YOUR SELF-KNOWLEDGE SCORE:

◯ /9 X 100 = ◯ %

II. STUDY SKILLS

I know how to...

◯ take notes from my reading assignments. (98)

◯ take complete notes in class that are useful to me when I study for exams. (99)

◯ identify what is important when I am reading. (102)

◯ organize my ideas and write and edit my own papers. (104)

◯ prepare for tests and final exams. (106)

( ) review my class notes, assigned readings, and other materials on a regular basis. (110)

( ) use the help available in school when I don't understand something or want to improve how I study. (111)

YOUR STUDY SKILLS SCORE:

( ) /21 X 100 = ( ) %

III. TIME MANAGEMENT

I can...

( ) set up my own study schedule. (112)

( ) consistently complete daily assigned homework. (113)

( ) develop a system for keeping track of due dates for all of my assignments. (115)

( ) stay on top of my reading assignments. (116)

( ) write assigned papers, study for tests, and complete long-term projects in a timely manner. (117)

YOUR TIME-MANAGEMENT SCORE:

( ) /15 X 100 = ( ) %

YOUR TOTAL ACADEMIC SKILLS SCORE:

( ) /45 X 100 = ( ) %

Now total the number of skills you rated 2 or lower: TOTAL = ( )

You will use this score on the Skills Analysis Worksheet that follows, which you should now complete.

STEP TWO: COMPLETE THE SKILLS ANALYSIS WORKSHEET

This worksheet is designed to help you target specific areas and skills that you need to develop before taking off to college. It will give you an idea of your strengths and weaknesses and help you plan for the time you have left in high school.

1. Which skill area is a strength for you (rated highest)? Add up the numbers and circle one of the skill areas listed below that corresponds to the highest score.

Self-Determination Skills
Self-knowledge | Self-advocacy | Self-management

Daily Living Skills
Self-care | Organization | Time management

Academic Skills
Self-knowledge | Study skills | Time management

2. Which skill area needs to improve the most? Add up the numbers and circle one that corresponds to the lowest score.

Self-Determination Skills
Self-knowledge | Self-advocacy | Self-management

Daily Living Skills
Self-care | Organization | Time management

Academic Skills
Self-knowledge | Study skills | Time management

3. Go back and look at the areas that you rated below 3.

How many of the skills did you rate 2 or lower?

4. Now count how many weeks until college begins. ( ) weeks.

Divide the total number of skills rated 2 or lower by the number of weeks left until college. This will give you an estimate of how many skills you should work on each week before college begins.

Total skills rated 2 or lower   /   number of weeks until college

If you had others rate you as well, look at their ratings and see what skills they think you already have and which ones they think you need to work on. How different is their list from yours?

If your ratings really disagree with the ratings of your parents and teachers, be courageous and have a discussion with them about why they made the ratings they did. If this seems too hard to do face-to-face, ask them to send you an email or write you a note explaining the reasons for their ratings. Consider averaging your ratings with the ratings of your parents and teachers and looking again at which skills you are best at and which skills you need to improve in the most. These ratings might be closer to what's happening in real life than your ratings in #1 and #2 above.

STEP THREE: WRITE SPECIFIC GOAL STATEMENTS

Setting clear, realistic goals for making a life change isn't as easy as it sounds. The more precise and specific we are about what we want to design in our lives, the more likely we are to use our conscious thought and energy to deliberately choose what we want to happen. If we have vague goals and plans, then our accomplishments may be as vague or our plans remain fuzzy and fail to materialize. Goals are best if they are specific, measurable, agreed to, realistic, and time-sensitive (**SMART**). A **SMART**, well-developed goal statement meets all the conditions listed here.

S = Specific: The more detail included in the goal, the better you'll be at focusing your efforts. Goals need to state very clearly what you want to accomplish.

M = Measurable: This ties in with the notion of being specific. A **SMART** goal statement is easy to measure so you can determine if you're making progress and can establish when you've succeeded.

A = Agreed To: There are several interpretations of the letter A in the acronym. One that we particularly like is that A means "Agreed To." This means that you've committed to taking action and aren't just complying to make others happy.

R = Realistic: Well-defined goals allow us to believe that we can, with different attitudes and behaviors, take the steps to make change happen. If goals are too easy or too lofty, it's hard to get motivated to take action.

T = Timely or Time Sensitive: A clear goal statement narrows the time frame for achievement. If you never take action because you're not defining an end point, you're condemning a goal to the realm of good intentions. Instead of saying "someday I will lose weight" a **SMART** goal-setter will say, "I will lose 5 pounds by graduation."

As you will discover, making a goal **SMART** will take some time and thought. Let's look at some examples of vague goals versus **SMART** goals and the differences between them.

This way of thinking and setting specific goals may be difficult initially. Be sure to ask for help or suggestions for both setting goals and creating an action plan (see pages 32–35 below) from a parent, therapist, or guidance counselor if you get stuck or are having difficulty at first. Eventually you'll become an expert at setting more specific, **SMART** goals for yourself. In the meantime, here's a worksheet to help you practice.

SMART GOALS VERSUS VAGUE GOALS

READINESS SKILL	VAGUE GOAL	SMART GOAL	DIFFERENCES
Self-Determination Skills: Self-Advocacy My score = 1	I want to be more social.	I will go out with friends or to an event 3 times each month.	The **SMART** goal is very targeted and will be easy to measure.
Daily Living Skills: Organization & Time Management My score = 1	I will go to bed earlier.	I will be in bed each school night no later than 11:30 PM.	In the vague goal, there could be debate about what earlier means, but not in the specific **SMART** goal.
Academic Skills: Study Skills My score = 1	I will study harder this grading period.	I will study 30 minutes daily, 5 days a week, for subjects where my grade is a C or lower.	The vague study goal can't be measured and the **SMART** goal is precise and realistic and the process will be easy to evaluate.

SMART GOALS WORKSHEET

WRITE A FIRST DRAFT OF YOUR GOAL	MAKE YOUR GOAL **MORE SPECIFIC**	MAKE YOUR GOAL **MEASUREABLE**	RATE WHETHER YOU HAVE FULLY **AGREED** TO OR COMMITTED TO YOUR GOAL (1=LOW COMMITMENT, 10=HIGH COMMITMENT) WHAT WILL HELP YOU AGREE TO YOUR GOAL?	RATE HOW **REALISTIC** YOUR GOAL IS (1=NOT VERY REALISTIC, 10=VERY REALISTIC) WHAT WILL MAKE YOUR GOAL MORE REALISTIC?	MAKE YOUR GOAL MORE **TIME SENSITIVE**	HOW WILL YOU **KNOW** IF YOU REACHED YOUR GOAL?
I will do more studying.	I will study more for French.	I will study two hours a day for French.	Agreed to Rating = 3 I will set up a system to reward myself for staying on track.	Realistic Rating = 3 I will study 30 minutes a day for French.	During the month of February, I will study 30 minutes a day for French from Monday through Thursday and once on the weekend.	I will keep a log of my study time using my cell phone.

EXAMPLE

YOUR TURN

Bachel, B. (2001). *What do you really want? How to set a goal and go for it!* A guide for teens. Minneapolis, MN: Free Spirit.

Covey, S. (1998). *The 7 habits of highly effective teens.* New York, NY: Franklin Covey.

Lifetick: **http://www.lifetick.com**. Lifetick is a very slick, web-based SMART goals tracker with free and paid versions and iCal and smartphone integration.

Joe's Goals: **http://www.joesgoals.com**. Joe's Goals is a simple, free goal tracking website.

42 Goals: **http://42goals.com**. This is another simple online tracker with a mobile version.

Stickk: **http://www.stickk.com**. Stickk is a funny little tool that lets you incentivize achieving your goals in a social way. You set a goal, and your friends and family can make monetary bets on whether you will achieve it. If you do, the money they've bet goes to a charity of your choosing.

STEP FOUR:
CREATE AN ACTION PLAN

Once you've written some very specific goal statements containing **SMART** goals for each skill that you are going to work on next, now is the time to focus on how you plan to reach these goals during the coming weeks. Questions to ask yourself include:

✔ What do you need to do? List the specific steps you will take to reach your goal.

✔ What support do you need from others?

✔ What resources will you need to reach your goal?

Printable CEO: **http://davidseah.com/productivity-tools**. You're probably not a high-powered corporate executive, but you can definitely find a way to use some of these printable project planners to help you put your action plan down on paper.

Use the Action Plan Worksheet

Creating an action plan, like setting goals, can be tough at first, but gets easier with practice. Here's a worksheet to get you started.

ACTION PLAN WORKSHEET

TIMEFRAME FOR MY ACTION PLAN: WEEK/MONTH OF _____

MY GOAL:

IS MY GOAL: SPECIFIC? MEASUREABLE? AGREED TO? REALISTIC? TIME SENSITIVE?

WHAT STEPS WILL I TAKE TO REACH MY GOAL?	WHEN WILL I TAKE EACH STEP?	WHAT MATERIALS, RESOURCES, OR SUPPORT DO I NEED TO HELP ME REACH MY GOAL?	HOW WILL I KNOW IF I COMPLETED THIS STEP?

STEP FIVE: DEVELOP A SYSTEM TO TRACK YOUR PROGRESS

Once you've created your plan, it's time to put it into action and start building your skills! But you'll also need a system to keep track of your progress. Determining how you will keep track of progress towards your goal is as important as setting the goal. Will you keep a chart, a log, or write in a planner? Be accountable to another person for your plan. Can you and a friend or adult have regular check-ins via Facebook? Email? Text messages? Face-to-face meetings? You're more likely to stick to your plan and achieve the goals you set earlier if someone else is holding you to it. Be sure to dip back into this book as you're working on each skill to make sure you're not forgetting any of the tips, resources, and advice.

STEP SIX: EVALUATE AND MODIFY YOUR PLAN

When you write your action plan, also set a date that is not too far in the future (2–3 weeks is best) when you will check to see if you have done what you said you would do and ask yourself if you've mastered the skill you've been working on. Review your progress and set new goals or rewrite your plan if needed.

By keeping track, maybe you've found out that you're great at setting goals, but not great about acting to achieve them. You may want to ask an adult or a friend to coach you. Make a commitment to this person and agree to check in as often as you need to help you do what you know you want to do. Tell this person how to respond if you forget to check in or don't take action. If possible, talk to you parents about finding you a professional in the school or community who can take on this coaching role.

Part II: Get Set

F irst, we want to encourage you use whatever time you have left in high school to get ready for college. Don't worry about how much time that is. While we realize that some of you may have only a few months and others may have a couple of years—any time that you devote to developing your skills will be useful and important to your success. You might even think about seeing if any of your friends would like to work on getting ready for college, too! If you have a high school guidance counselor or special education class teacher who you like and trust, ask him or her to get involved and help you create a plan to get ready.

Second, as you develop your action plans for each skill you are working on, there is no need to continue to read this guide in a certain order or from start to finish. Instead, the chapters on the various skills sets and individual skills that follow are provided as a resource for you. They are like a menu. You pick and choose. What section you read next will depend on the skill you have chosen to work on. We encourage you to reread particular sections a few times while you're practicing your skills to make sure you're getting the most out of this time.

Third, remember that change is always difficult and if you have parents who have always done everything for you (like the parents we talked about previously on pages 13–14) then now is the time to have a serious discussion with them about collaborating on this action plan. Be sure to present your reasoning for wanting to change in a positive way and show them this book or refer them to others we have presented in this guide. If you feel that they don't understand why you want to make these changes now, you may need to ask for help explaining your plan from a trusted teacher or guidance counselor at your high school. If your parents (and teachers) are on board and have read this guide (or the book **Ready for Take-Off: Preparing Your Teen With ADHD or LD for College,** which we wrote specifically for them) then begin meeting regularly to develop the skills that you identified on the checklist as needing work.

The next three Skill Set chapters (Part II of this guide) contain tips, tools, and resources to help you develop the specific skills you need to work on before going off to college. These tips are presented in the same order they appeared on the checklist. Each chapter focuses on one skill set, and includes tips and resources for each specific skill within that set. For example, if you found that you need to work on your Self-Advocacy and Communication Skills and specifically on getting better at admitting when you don't understand and asking for help, tips for this skill can be found on page 50 in the Self-Determination Skills chapter of the guide. The skill set is in the gray box on the outside of the pages. The specific skill is along the top of the page.

Reread the tips provided in these chapters as often as you need to in order to come up with a specific action plan that works, and don't forget to ask for ideas from others—including your parents, teachers, and friends. You can also check out the Books and Bookmarks lists included throughout to find print and web resources that might provide more help or additional strategies.

Self-Determination Skills

SELF-KNOWLEDGE

Many experts agree that successful transitions to college require that teens with ADHD/LD be knowledgeable about themselves. Building self-awareness is a process that includes reflecting on yourself and your experiences, getting feedback from others, thinking about this feedback, and having discussions with others.

The first step in developing self-awareness is for you to gain an accurate and thorough understanding of your talents, strengths, and interests, as well as any weaknesses, including your diagnosed disability and how it impacts your functioning. It can take a lifetime to really figure this all out! Because you are, and will continue to be, the main person responsible for yourself, now is the time to make sure that you really are starting to see the complete picture.

Talents, Interests, and Dreams for the Future

Once in college, you will be presented with many opportunities that require self-knowledge about your talents and interests (not just academic strengths), weaknesses, and a thorough understanding of your disabilities. You will eventually have to select a college major and pursue a career path. To make these types of decisions effectively, you need to know more about what you enjoy and are naturally inclined to do. Here are some ideas to get you started.

✔ **Find your passion.** Think about the things that you loved to do when you were younger and continue to enjoy. Ask your parents for their input.

✔ **Analyze your free time.** When you have free time, what fills that time? Keep a daily or weekly log and list your activities during free time and rate them for interest and enjoyment. Sometimes, experiments in self-observation like this one provide great insight.

✔ **Look at past misbehaviors.** Sometimes strengths, talents, and interests can get kids in trouble because they engage in activities that they are passionate about (or that come naturally) when parents or teachers don't want them to. Think about the things that you did that got you into trouble. For example: Did you read books under the covers late into the night or hide them in boring school books in class? Did you doodle and draw all over the nice, new notebooks you bought? Are you always helping neighbors do chores instead of doing chores around the house? Think about what talents and interests might be hidden under these misbehaviors.

✔ **Look for patterns.** Talents, strengths, and interests can also show up as patterns in school and may lead to trouble when there are rules and schedules with times dedicated to specific activities. So, gather up all your old report cards and look for patterns. What comments did teachers make? For example, if all your teachers said you talked too much to your friends, then maybe you are a natural communicator or leader. Once again, be curious and ask yourself what talents might be behind these misbehaviors.

✔ **Assess your talents and interests.** Use published or online surveys that assess your talents and interests. Strengthsquest, referenced in our Books and Bookmarks section below, is one such survey that is geared to helping high schoolers and college-aged youth uncover their natural strengths and talents. Of course these surveys can't fully capture a person's talents, but they can get you started thinking more about yourself.

✔ **Meet with your high school guidance counselor.** See what inventories, surveys, or activities might be available to help you get more information about natural talents and interests. These might be included in workshops or classes on career exploration.

✔ **Experiment with new activities.** This is a great way to see if you might uncover a hidden talent or interest. For example, join a Saturday art or theatre class, join the church youth choir, or volunteer at a retirement home. Volunteer for extracurricular activities at school or service organizations in the community. By trying out different types of experiences, you may get a clearer idea of your talents and interests.

Chang, R. (2000). *The passion plan: A step-by-step guide to discovering, developing and living your passion.* San Francisco, CA: Jossey-Bass.

Covey, S. (1998). *The 7 habits of highly effective teens.* New York, NY: Franklin Covey.

Strengthsquest: **http://www.strengthsquest.com**. This online survey assesses talents and interests.

Getting Used to New People, Places, and Situations

Being ready for college depends in large part on how well you can adjust to life in a new and unfamiliar setting. Will you become homesick for family, friends, and the high school where things were so familiar and structured? Will you dive in head-first and experience all of the freedom and opportunity of college life? Or will your adjustment to college life be somewhere in between these two extremes? Many college students are surprised to find that they were more homesick than they thought they would be.

Experts agree that there are some common styles of reacting to change. No one temperamental style is good or bad, but all styles have up- and downsides. A person who welcomes change may always be seeking new experiences and not think critically about the challenges that she might encounter as she gets involved in too many activities. While the student who retreats from change may take longer to connect and find her way, she may be more realistic about the problems that adjusting to a new environment may produce.

Whatever your style of reacting to change, going to college is one of the most challenging adjustments you will have to face. You've already spent some time thinking about all the new things that you have to adapt to at college. Before you even head off to college, it might really help if you and your parents had a look at your typical response to change.

The adjustment you're preparing for may be challenging for your parents as well. It might help to discuss with them now the idea of your being on your own and away at school and their reactions to this new situation. That way, they will understand and support your need to work on some of these skills now, even if it means a few bumps along the way as you learn to do things for yourself.

Use the questions below to start thinking about your style of reacting to changes.

✓ **Look at old patterns.** First, think back on the many transitions you and your parents have already experienced. Talk about how you adjusted to kindergarten, middle school, high school, camp, moving into a new house, going to a new church, joining a new club, etc. What patterns do you both see as your typical response to these changes?

✓ **Analyze current responses.** Whenever a new situation presents itself, use it as an opportunity to reflect on your response style. What did you feel like at a party where everyone was a stranger? What about at the dance at school?

✓ **Look at past success.** What have you done in the past to help adjust to a new situation?

✓ **Think about future challenges.** How do you think you might feel and react during the adjustment to college? Make predictions based on what you have learned about your behaviors in the past.

Many teens, even those without disabilities, find the college adjustment period to be very difficult. Find out if any of your local colleges have special transition programs for high school students to help them slowly get ready for college. Sometimes these programs allow teens to live on a college campus for a week or so in the summer. Students can see what dorm life is like, have a simulated college class, and be mentored by veteran students. Here are some more ideas you might consider trying:

✓ **Visit college campuses.** If you have relatives or friends in college, see if you can visit them, stay overnight, and attend a class or two. Or see if campuses nearby have programs for high school students to tour campus, spend the night in a dorm, and visit a class.

✓ **Get a head start.** Once you have been accepted to a specific college, ask about summer bridge experiences that might be available. These experiences are typically available for minority students, first generation students, or students from smaller high schools. Find out who is in charge of this program and ask if you can apply. Programs like these are invaluable for increasing success in the first important semester of college when so many teens struggle.

✓ **Create your own summer program.** If the college you select doesn't have a summer bridge program, create your own. You can do this and get a head start by enrolling in the last session of summer school. Have the Department of Disability Services review your documentation before summer school or as soon as you are accepted. That way, you will be able to get the accommodations you need while taking one or two classes in the summer when the campus is typically less frantic. Making your own summer transition program can allow you to test out college in a quieter environment with fewer class demands and to get familiar with campus, dorm life, and with the procedures for using accommodations and accessing resources on campus.

Understanding Your Strengths and Weaknesses in Academic and Learning Skills

It is possible that your parents may have a better sense than you do of your academic and learning skills—after all, your parents have been focusing on you for longer than you've been alive. If you're not sure about your strengths and weaknesses in these areas, the activities and questions below can help you develop a more specific understanding of where you excel, where you need to work harder, and how your disability impacts your learning.

✓ **Take a look at your old report cards.** You might even read them over with your parents. Look at the teachers' comments. What positive comments did teachers seem to mention from year to year? What academic strengths might these comments match? What negative comments were consistently mentioned and what academic skills might be behind these more negative evaluations? Is it possible that your disability was the culprit? Look for patterns in your grades. In which classes did you do well and in which did you struggle? To identify weaknesses, think specifically about things that you dislike or have trouble doing. Why are these tasks difficult for you? Think about subjects at school and tasks at home that you avoid at all costs. Do these give you a clue about your weaknesses?

✓ **Understand your disability.** Do you really understand your disability and how it affects you academically? Or do you just have a vague or general understanding of it? For example, do you say things like: "I have an auditory processing problem" or "I have a non-verbal learning disability" and not really know what they mean? If you can't state specifically how your disability affects you at school, at home, and socially, then you need to dig deeper.

✓ **Ask to see the written report from the evaluation when you were diagnosed and read it together with your parents, the person who diagnosed you, or the resource specialist at school.** Talk it over. Make a list of what you are learning and make another list of any questions that you might have. This may include terms you don't really understand or things that you (or your parents) are wondering about as you read the report.

✓ **Interview your parents.** Ask them to share what they see as your strengths and weaknesses and find out how they think these have affected you over the years.

✓ **Ask to meet with someone at your school who can go over your written report with you.** Perhaps you need a meeting with the special class teacher, the transition specialist, or the school psychologist. Ask this person to help you understand how your disability shows up or affects you in school, at home, and socially. When you don't understand what they're saying, be bold and ask for a clear explanation. Consider recording this meeting so you and your parents can listen to the explanation again later.

✓ **Conduct an Internet search to learn more about your disability.** There are tons of websites that specialize in information on ADHD or LD. Check out some of the ones we've listed below and find some on your own.

SELF-DETERMINATION SKILLS

GENERAL INFORMATION ABOUT LD

Learning Disabilities Association of America:
http://www.ldanatl.org.

LD Online: http://www.ldonline.org.

LD Resources: http://www.ldresources.org.

GENERAL INFORMATION ABOUT ADHD

ADDvance: http://addvance.com.

Attention Deficit Disorder Resources:
http://www.addresources.org.

CHADD: http://www.chadd.org.

Dr. Hallowell: http://www.drhallowell.com/add-adhd.

ADDitude: http://www.additudemag.com

HEATH Resource Center: http://www.heath.gwu.edu. The HEATH Resource Center is an online clearinghouse on postsecondary education for individuals with disabilities. It has lots of articles and information.

Mooney, J. and Cole, D. (2000). *Learning outside the lines*. New York, NY: Fireside.

Quinn, P.O. (2001). *ADD and the college student*. Washington, DC: Magination Press.

Nadeau, K. (2006). *Survival guide for college students with ADHD or LD*, 2nd edition. Washington, DC: Magination Press.

SELF-ADVOCACY AND COMMUNICATION SKILLS

After unloading all of your possessions into your dorm room and waving goodbye to your parents, you will immediately need to start using your self-advocacy skills. What will you do when there is a discussion about who gets which bed and desk in the dorm room? How will you handle it when you get an email telling you to go to the financial aid office before classes begin to work out the terms of your student loan?

In addition, you will have to use these skills to activate the services and accommodations available to you. What will you do when the Department of Disability Services sends out an email telling all newly cleared students to call or drop by to make an appointment to arrange accommodations? What about making phone calls to make appointments for meeting a local doctor to get a prescription, or going to campus health when you are sick? How will you talk with professors to arrange getting class notes or extended time for exams? What will you say when your classmates ask where you were the day of the exam? Here are some ideas to help you practice this skill.

✓ **Make a folder that will go with you to college.** It needs to include a copy of your most recent testing report and written answers to the following questions: What are my strengths and my weaknesses? What is my disability? When was it diagnosed? How does it impact my learning? How does it impact me in other areas of my life? What accommodations or modifications do I need to help me compensate for my disability? You should also practice responding to these questions orally.

✓ **Decide on your learning style and strategies that you know help you learn better.** (See pages 93–96 for more on identifying how you learn best and developing strategies that suit your style.)

✓ **Take advantage of every opportunity for you to self-advocate instead of asking or allowing your parents or teachers to jump**

in for you. Are you attending your IEP (Individualized Education Plan) or 504 Meetings at school? If you have a regular class teacher who doesn't understand your needs, fight the temptation to have your parents or your special class teacher do the talking. Instead, you can make an appointment to talk with this teacher and explain the difficulties you are having. At first you might want your parents or your special education teacher to practice with you and role-play how the conversation might go. You might even ask them to attend the meeting for moral support. But make sure you do most of the talking.

✓ **Stop having your parents make calls to doctors, hair appointments, and pharmacies, and make them yourself.** You might hate it, but you'll have to do it someday. Write out a script before you pick up the phone, even if you're calling for something as simple as a hair appointment. Ask your parents what they usually say when they make those calls. They might think this task is easy, but if you've never called your doctor before, you might not know what to expect. You might even want to role-play the call with them or a friend.

Unfortunately, most of the tools out there for promoting these communication skills are written for teachers or parents, but that doesn't mean you can't check them out and translate them to your own situation.

Parents' Guide to Transition. **http://www.heath.gwu.edu/modules/** parents-guide-to-transition. In addition to explaining self-advocacy, this article explains the differences in the laws governing college and those governing the public schools and the important roleof the young adult in obtaining accommodations and services.

Introducing Yourself to New People and Carrying On a Conversation

One of the top skills any new college student needs is the ability to meet new people, start conversations, and keep them going. Once again, depending upon your temperament and disability, these skills might be a no brainer. On the other hand, these skills may be overwhelmingly difficult for you. If you're more introverted, you may find it difficult to enter a room or go to an event where you don't know anyone else and initiate a conversation—even if you know how to have a conversation. Some teens with ADHD/LD notice that the give and take of conversation can be very painful, as they take longer to interpret what others say and have to pause for a longer time to respond. Other teens with ADHD who are outgoing may have the opposite problem and overwhelm strangers by monopolizing conversations and sharing more than the listener can handle. Sound familiar? Don't worry—practice may not make perfect, but it really does make talking to people easier.

✔ **Be open to meeting new people.** Look for opportunities to be in groups with unfamiliar people of all ages and try out some of your conversation skills.

✔ **Practice talking and listening and keeping the conversation going.** Set very specific goals for yourself, like "I will introduce myself to three new people at the party Friday night and hold a several-minute conversation with each," or "I will ask each person I talk to two questions about themselves."

✔ **Develop a list of conversation starters.** Favorite websites, video games, movies, sports, television shows, school, and vacations are things lots of people like to talk about. Work on ways to keep conversations going by asking more questions, sharing a comment, or using non-verbal cues like head nodding that show interest.

✔ **Use the resources available at school or in the community.** Does the school counselor have any material to help with this skill? Is there a speech and language specialist at school who can help you develop the skills to start and hold conversations? Are there any classes on this skill at a local community college or center?

Expressing Your Strengths and Weaknesses Clearly

It will be critical for you to be able to explain your strengths and weaknesses and how your disability affects learning. Being able to name and ask for the accommodations that help you compensate is also crucial. See the tips for improving self-advocacy skills at college on pages 47–48 for ways to practice while still in high school.

Admitting When You Don't Understand and Asking for Help

At college, you will need to recognize when it is time to seek help and then find the resources you need. In the meantime, while you are still in high school, be on the lookout. Chances are, sooner or later you'll encounter a challenge that you can't deal with by persistence alone. Practice identifying the appropriate resource person at school or in the community, and ask for help. This is the time to start to notice the feelings or warning signs that tell you you're meeting limited success trying to solve a problem on your own. For example:

- Are you **confused** and having **difficulty understanding** a concept being taught in class?

- Are you getting behind in your assignments and starting to feel **stressed** and **panicky?**

- Do you find yourself in a social situation that makes you **uncomfortable?**

- Do you feel **frustrated** with a particular task or assignment?

- Are you **unsure** about the next step to take to solve a problem?

- Are you feeling **stuck** because you are working on the same problem or rereading the same materials over and over and not getting anywhere?

These feelings could all be signs that you need to ask for help, and using resources is the way to handle this problem instead of trying harder on your own.

Finding the Help and Support You Need

When you are experiencing one or more of the feelings we mentioned above, ask yourself, who at school might be the appropriate person to talk with about the challenge I'm facing? Or, is there anyone else I know who could help me? Once the resource person is identified, talk with this person and explain what help you need. In college, you will need to work smarter, not harder. Here are some ways to find help:

✔ **Search your high school website** to learn about all the available resources.

✔ **Check in with your health professional.** If you are having problems or side effects from any medications, take these concerns to the right person. That's usually the person who prescribes or oversees the medication. Make a list of your concerns. Be sure to rehearse beforehand what you want to say during the phone call or meeting.

✔ **Find resources at the college you will be attending.** As you get closer to going away to college, search that college's website to find all the resources available for the various issues you might face. These could be related to problems that crop up while living in the dorm, health issues, emotional or relationship problems, or the need for academic supports and disability services. Bookmark these sites and talk about when and how to use these resources with a parent, teacher, or counselor at school.

Expressing Your Thoughts and Standing Firm When You Have a Differing Opinion

Being able to disagree with friends, expressing a differing opinion, and standing up for what you believe in are all important skills that you need throughout your life. If standing up for yourself and defending your opinion is a problem for you, try to practice these skills as often as you can in high school—maybe even role-playing with a parent or older sibling if necessary.

✔ Consider joining the debate team or speech club, if your high school has one; you'll gain lots of useful tips and pointers for expressing yourself clearly.

✔ You might also visit websites that provide information on how to communicate a difference of opinion assertively or for suggestions on ways to effectively disagree with someone else.

✔ Your guidance counselor or special class teacher may have information on being assertive.

✔ If you find it extremely distressing to stand up for your views, consider that you might need to get some professional counseling or therapy. Don't be afraid to get the help you need now to allow yourself to become more confident and assertive before college when your parents won't be around to make the rules that sometimes help you say "no" to friends.

One very real situation that many students with ADHD face at college is having other students pressure them for stimulant medication so that they can study for exams or write papers. In today's world, using medication to improve performance is something lots of college students without ADHD do. It takes courage to say "no" to another person, but the self-respect you'll feel after you do is well worth the discomfort. If the other person really is your friend, she will respect you and the limits you set. And, remember, it is illegal to sell or distribute controlled substances. One time could land you in a lot of trouble; and besides, if you sell or give away your medication, how will you pay attention and get your work done?

Talk with your parents or your doctor about the possibility of being approached for stimulants and come up with some ideas of what you can say if the situation arises. If it is going on right now in high school, you may need to talk with the school counselor or nurse to let them know what is happening so you don't have to handle this alone. These same ideas will work in college as well. There are Resident Assistants in college dorms who can help you, and the doctors and counselors at university counseling centers can help teens who are being asked for their medication.

Hopkins, L. (2009). *6 tips for effective use of assertive communication.* Retrieved from **http://ezinearticles.com/?Assertive-Communication—6-Tips-For-Effective-Use&id=10259**

Communication Skills: **http://www.pamf.org/teen/abc/building blocks/communication.html**. This site gives some great ideas for many of the important communication skills we have talked about in this section.

Talking About and Handling Conflict

While you've almost certainly experienced conflict at home and at school, you may not have learned how to effectively disagree and continue sticking to your beliefs in the way you will need to when you're on your own at college. Many people of all ages have difficulty handling conflict. If you find that this is an area of weakness for you, now's the time to get help. Here are a few ideas to help improve this skill.

✔ **Visit websites** that provide information on how to handle conflict, like the "Communication Skills" page here: **http://www.pamf.org/teen/abc/buildingblocks/communication.html**.

✔ **Consult the school guidance counselor** to see if she has materials on this topic.

✔ **Role-play** your part in the conversation with a friend or parent or write out your thoughts ahead of time.

✔ **Use "I" messages.** Express your thoughts using "I" messages that clearly express **your** feelings. For example, if you are upset that your friend is always joking about your getting extended time for tests, instead of responding with a "you" message like, "You make me mad when you tease me like that," you can turn the sentence around by saying what you feel and why, starting the sentence with the word "I." You could say, "I don't like it when you constantly tease me about getting extended time. It makes me feel disappointed because I hope that my good friends understand that I have a difference that makes me read more slowly and I can't help it." By using an "I" message, you can say what you feel in a way that the other person might hear it.

✔ **Listen first, talk second.** To solve a problem effectively, you have to understand where the other person is coming from before defending your own position.

✔ **Set out the facts.** Agree and establish the objective, observable elements that will have an impact on the discussion and any decisions you might make.

✔ **Explore options to resolve the conflict together.** Be open to the idea that a third position may exist, and that you can get to this idea jointly.

Participating in Class Discussions or Groups

With fewer exams and quizzes, grades in college are often even more dependent on class participation. Some seminar classes can be discussion *only* without formal lectures. Sometimes students are assigned to work in groups on class projects. If you are shy or this is a weak area for you, now is the time to build this skill. Try one or all of the following ideas to get you started.

✔ **Keep up-to-date.** Make sure you have read and have completed all assignments.

✔ **Prepare ahead of time.** Read the syllabus or ask the teacher to find out what will be covered in the next class. Read up on it in the text and go to the Web to get additional interesting, related information. When you meet with a group for a class assignment, go prepared and think about how you want to contribute to the assignment.

✔ **Write it down.** Write out a script, jot down some thoughts, or prepare an outline to help you organize the material you have just read. Refer to your notes during class or group meetings.

✔ **Work to overcome shyness.** If you are shy, preparing and rehearsing what you want to say may help. Discussing the topic you're studying or working on with a friend or another student from the class, a parent, or an older sibling might also help you feel more prepared and confident.

✔ **Talk to your teacher.** In college, if your grade depends on your class participation, your professor needs to know that talking in class is a challenge for you, and that it's something you're working on. Talk to your high school teachers to practice talking to professors. Be careful how you frame this discussion. "I want to make sure I do well and I'm excited to work on participation in class, but it's hard for me and it would really help if you could tell me when I need to do a better job of speaking up" will probably sound better to a professor than, "Just so you know, participating in class is something I'm not very good at, so I hope you can keep that in mind when you're assigning grades." You might also ask the teacher if he would be willing to call on you only when your hand is up, because that means that you have organized and prepared what you will say. Or ask if you can talk one-on-one to show that you are keeping up with the class.

SELF-MANAGEMENT

Regularly Setting Realistic Goals

This skill and the next one on creating an action plan are critical to success in all areas of your life—not just at college. We have already provided lots of information for developing these skills on pages 29–35. Here are some additional ideas for practicing these important skills.

✔ **Look for opportunities for goal-setting and action-planning.** When weekends roll around or there are longer vacations from school, think about what you would like to accomplish or enjoy during the downtime and generate a plan to achieve these short-term goals.

✔ **Look at some of your passions and interests** and practice setting goals to further explore or develop these areas that you may have had to neglect because of school.

✔ **Look for different ways to reach your goals.** Brainstorm possible ideas for implementing your goal by asking questions like, "What might help me reach this goal?" or "What would work best for me in this situation?" "What has worked in similar situations in the past?" Ask friends or siblings what they do when they are in this situation.

✔ **Ask others for their observations** of what they have noticed seems to work for you in reaching your goals.

✔ **Use this guide.** Look up the skill you are working on and read those pages to see if any of the tips and resources provided might be of use.

✔ **Think about future steps.** What will you need to do to accomplish what you have decided? What do you need to do to put your new idea into place? What will help you remember to take these steps? And what role, if any, would you like your parent or others to play in your action plan?

Developing Plans and Putting Them Into Action

In order to reach your goals, you must now know how to develop an action plan that will ensure that you are on track for success. You must also know how to evaluate and modify the plan if necessary. The worksheet provided on page 34 will help you create an action plan. That section also contains ways to evaluate your progress and modify your plan if necessary.

Thinking About Progress and Making Modifications

If you need to work on looking critically at your progress and reevaluating your action plan, the best thing you can do is to start writing. Write out your goals and your action plan using the worksheets on pages 31 and 34. If your goals and your plan are in writing (or on the computer) they're there for you to check on and change. See page 35 of this guide, also, for more tips.

Dealing With Challenges Without Feeling Frustrated

Managing yourself requires that you manage the full range of emotions and frustrations that are a regular part of life. It's common for teens with ADHD/LD, however, to have very low frustration tolerance. A lot of students with ADHD/LD abandon plans at the first sign of trouble or get totally derailed by their feelings. If that sounds like you, try the following tips to help you handle frustration better.

✔ **Take a break.** If you are particularly frustrated, try walking away and coming back to the problem later when you are calmer and can think more clearly. Do you think that it might help if you go for a walk or listen to music? Then you can come back with a fresh attitude and see how things go. Maybe taking a break right now is the best way to handle things.

✔ **Ask for help.** No one said you needed to tackle everything alone. Some-times just having someone to sit with helps you to remain calm and keep at a project or problem until you've solved it.

✔ **Sleep on it.** Many problems that seem huge when you are tired seem much more manageable in the morning after a good night's rest.

✔ **Look for the positive.** Often it's difficult, but you usually can find some-thing positive in each situation, and a positive mind is more open to finding a solution.

✔ **Keep at it. Don't give up.** You'll feel good about yourself for trying even if you don't succeed completely.

✔ **Come up with a list of questions** that you can use to help you unravel your emotions whenever you are feeling frustrated. Asking yourself, "What feelings am I noticing in my body right now and why might I feel this way?" may be helpful in clarifying these situations. Feelings can be messages from you to yourself that tell you to change what you are doing. So think about the information these feelings are giving you. What is the problem right now? What options do you have for dealing with it? How can you break the problem down into manageable steps?

✔ **Break a problem down into more manageable steps.** Think about the smaller steps you need to take to achieve the bigger thing that is making you frustrated or stressed out. Try to make the pieces as small as possible, focus on accomplishing them one by one, and be sure to acknowledge when you've accomplished even the smallest step.

Observing and Dealing With Emotions, Attention, and Behavior

Being on your own means successfully managing strong emotions as well as noticing whether you are on task and if you are paying attention to what you intended. This type of self-management requires that you have the ability to observe what is going on and to think about how to redirect yourself if things aren't going so well. Many college students, even those without ADHD/LD, struggle with becoming sidetracked by strong emotions or other distractions and have difficulty remaining on task. Try the following activities to help you develop better control as you are working on this skill.

✔ **Notice when you have a strong emotion or reaction to something.** Try to analyze what is really going on. Don't minimize your feelings, but try to look dispassionately at the situation—almost as though it were happening to someone else. Ask yourself, "What am I noticing right now and why do I think this is happening?"

✔ **Ask yourself questions to encourage problem solving:** "What can I or someone else do to help me deal with this feeling?" or "How can I deal with this situation in a better way right now?"

✔ **Focus on what you want to happen.** Sometimes we get so wrapped up in our emotions we forget what we were originally trying to accomplish.

✔ **Remember, you always have options of how you will choose to react.** Stop for a minute, take one or two deep breaths, and then **choose** how you are going to handle this particular situation, rather than just reacting.

✔ **Analyze what is getting in the way.** If you struggle with being on task when you set aside time to study, then think critically about what is getting in your way and what would help you. Some students intentionally leave their laptops and other technology in their dorm room and go to a different location without any computers, TVs, or MP3 players around when they want to study. Some reward themselves and after 50 minutes of studying they give themselves 10 minutes with the technology of their choice. Others have downloaded free software that allows them to block their internet access.

How can I deal with my anger? Retrieved from **http://kidshealth.org /teen/your_mind/emotions/deal_with_anger.html.**

Doerflinger, L. (2009). *Anger management for teens: Self help steps to control your emotions.* Retrieved from **http:// www.associatedcontent.com/article/1407294/anger_ management_for_teens_self_help.html?cat=72**

Freedom: **http://macfreedom.com.** Freedom prevents you from accessing the Internet for up to eight hours at a time and is a favorite of folks who write novels. It's available for all operating systems.

Vitamin R: **http://www.publicspace.net/Vitamin-R.** If the computer-installed Solitaire is a distraction for you, just blocking the Internet won't do much good. Vitamin R can block software or downloaded applications that are problematic.

Self Control: **http://visitsteve.com/made/selfcontrol.** Self Control is a Mac-only application that will block your ability to go to specified websites for a period of time.

Listening and Understanding
Without Getting Defensive

It's difficult to listen to someone talking about you or something that you have done without getting defensive. No one wants to listen to things about themselves that appear to threaten their sense of identity. It's easy to lash out or shut down in these circumstances. If you tend to have difficulty in this area, try the following tips to learn to listen and understand with an open mind.

✓ **Start by thinking about the person who is talking to you.** Most likely she is just trying to be helpful. She probably cares about you a lot, or she wouldn't be confronting you directly about this issue. Try to remember how much courage it took for her to bring up this subject and that it must be important to her or for you to hear.

✓ **Pay attention to your body language.** Try to relax as you listen. This will send the right message—that you are interested and aren't angry—to the other person, and it will make you more available to process the information. Look for signs that you might be getting upset. Are you tightening your stomach, clenching your fists or your jaw, or feeling stressed? If so, try taking a few slow, deep breaths to relax. If this is a consistent problem for you, try to practice relaxation techniques like slow breathing or muscle relaxation when you're not upset, so that you'll be able to call on those skills when you are.

✓ **Change your perspective.** Remember that the other person is watching your life from afar, and might be able to see parts of yourself that you haven't been able to see. It's like how you can use a mirror to see the back of your head—you can use this person to see something that's usually out of sight. Use the opportunity to learn about yourself and see yourself as others see you. Instead of getting defensive, see what you can learn from the other person's comments.

✓ **Be careful not to respond without thinking.** Practice not interrupting and allowing yourself time to think before responding to a statement. Talk to the people in your life about techniques you can use to remind yourself to take that time. If you lash back immediately, in most cases you will regret it later. Take some time to think about what the other person said. Was there any truth to it? What do you need or want to do in response?

✔ **Be polite.** Offering a sincere "thank you" or an "I'll think about that" may be the most appropriate response, and it gives you time to think about what you heard and evaluate your response if one is needed.

Prochaska, J. O., Norcross, J. C., & DiClemente, C. C. (1994). *Changing for good: A revolutionary six-stage program for overcoming bad habits and moving your life positively forward.* New York, NY: William Morrow.

Communication Skills: **http://www.pamf.org/teen/abc/building-blocks/communication.html**. This site gives some great ideas for many of the important communication skills we have talked about in this section. Check out all the great information under the general head of "Communication Skills, Eight Things to Practice and Tough Conversations."

Asking Questions or Asking to Have Information Repeated

In high school, your teacher may have encouraged you to ask questions if you didn't understand the material taught in class. However, professors in college may not entertain questions and certainly do not expect to repeat information covered in the text. Some classes have specific sessions led by teacher's assistants (TAs) where a student can come to ask questions, but TAs don't often reteach the material.

Professors may schedule office hours for students to come in and discuss a specific issue, but these sessions aren't always very frequent. Also, classes often move fast, and it can be hard to sneak in a question. In order to practice getting the most out of your time in class and to become expert at asking questions when you need to, we have the following suggestions for you to try while in high school.

- **Practice finding the answers yourself.** Spend a class writing down any questions that come to mind as your teacher is speaking, then look for ways to get these questions answered. Is the material in the text? Would calling a classmate help? Can you find the information online or in the syllabus for the class? Has the material been covered in a previous class?

- **Set up a separate meeting outside of class.** Schedule a meeting with the teacher and ask if you could spend a few minutes before or after class to have her answer questions or clear up any confusion about the material covered.

- **Set up a study group.** Try to set up a peer study group with a few of your friends from the class. This is a great way to go over the material and get your questions answered.

- **Set guidelines for asking questions or speaking up in class.** If you do need to ask a question in class, be brief and as concise as possible. You might want to acknowledge that you're interrupting the flow of the class and thank the teacher for giving you the time and an answer. Also, make sure that what you are asking or saying is matched to the class or group discussion. Some students have a tendency to share too much or bring in material that is not related to the discussion. Take care and monitor yourself by asking, "Is this relevant to the topic?" before you ask a question in class.

- **Restate for clarification.** Sometimes briefly stating the material as it was presented may help clear up a confusing point for you and other students as well. For example, "Are you saying that . . . is the result of . . . ?"

- **Be respectful.** Always remember to be polite and do not try to show off. It's important to show the teacher that you're working hard, but it can be easy to go overboard, especially if you're already inclined to share what you know with others. Think about whether what you're saying is really adding to the lesson, so you don't get an unearned reputation for being a show-off or teacher's pet.

✔ **Consider recording the class.** If you do have trouble listening and understanding, it may help you to get permission to use a digital recorder or some other recording technology, like the Livescribe pen mentioned on page 101. These devices will allow you to listen to the lecture later and hear what you missed. Then, if you still have questions, you can talk to the teacher individually later without affecting the class.

SELF-DETERMINATION SKILLS

Daily Living Skills

Developing strong daily living skills is crucial if you are going to be fully ready for life on your own at college. Suddenly being responsible for taking care of yourself at the same time that you are making the social and academic adjustments college requires can be overwhelming. Even if you aren't thrilled about learning these skills now, try to think about how much easier your first months on your own will be because you were responsible in high school. Chores will always be chores, but they don't have to be overwhelming or opportunities for disaster.

Your parents may not realize how much they are involved in helping with these various daily activities, especially if they fit one of those patterns we described on page 13-14. To really gain independence, you might need to help your parents realize that they need to allow you to assume responsibility for these skills and to face some consequences now, before you are on your own at college. The book that we wrote especially for them, **Ready for Take-Off**, is full of information to help your parents make this adjustment with you.

SELF-CARE

Washing and Caring for Your Own Clothes

Have you ever had to deal with the consequences of using hot water with the wrong fabric or color, or forgetting to empty tissues out of your pockets? Even your mom or perfect older brother has probably turned white clothes pink or been upset to pull out of the dryer a wool sweater that shrunk to the size of a hand puppet. It happens to the best of us when we are in a hurry.

However, these mishaps may happen consistently if you don't learn how to do laundry on your own before you leave for college. Unless you have the resources to pay for a laundry service on campus or plan on bringing tons of dirty clothes home when you return for a visit, you need to learn how to keep up with laundry. The organizational piece of doing laundry can be tough if you have problems due to your ADHD/LD. We hope that the following ideas will be helpful.

✓ **Find an approach to learning laundry basics that matches your learning style.** Would it be best to do an Internet search and read about laundry? Watch a video? There are tons available online specifically for college students. Or would a demonstration work best? If so, by whom? An older sibling? Cousin? Relative?

✓ **First, concentrate on washing.** No matter how you choose to instruct yourself, you need to learn about washing first. Find out how and why it's important to sort clothes; empty pockets; and select different water temperatures, load sizes, cycles, and detergents. You can even find out which clothes *don't* need to be washed after every wear—you don't want to wear your jeans until they can stand up without you in them, but most people agree that you can come pretty darn close.

✓ **Then, get the drying down.** Unless you want to wear wet clothes, you also need some information about the dryer, including: What do the different settings mean? Why should you clean the filter? What kinds of clothes should you hang to dry instead of tossing in a hot dryer?

Set a date. Talk with your parents and decide on the actual date when they will stop being involved in doing your laundry. To avoid later conflicts and nagging, it's also good to decide in advance what role, if any, you want them to play if they notice that your laundry is piling up.

Taking Medications

Whether you take medication for acne, allergies, asthma, diabetes, ADHD, or other psycological issues like depression or anxiety, you need to know what to do on a daily basis to stay on top of your medical needs.

At college, we've seen teens stop following doctors' orders or skip recommended treatments because they haven't fully accepted that they need medication. If you're not sure you should be on your medications, the earlier you can get to the bottom of your real needs, the better. Here are several tips to help you understand your medical needs and become skilled in taking care of any health issues.

 Take the lead. Begin by taking the lead at doctor's appointments related to your health issues. The goal is to make sure you understand your health issues and are adequately informed about any necessary medical treatments. Prior to appointments, think about what you don't understand and make a list of any questions to ask at the appointment.

 Discuss the reason for your treatments. If you're not sure you really need a medicine you've been prescribed, schedule a three-way meeting with your healthcare professional and your parents to explain your concerns and to ask for clarifications. Your healthcare provider is the one who can best guide you and offer reasons why you need to take a certain medication or treatment. If you have a serious health issue, it may not be wise to totally refuse treatment, but be sure you have all the facts before you make such a serious decision. If you feel like you have made significant improvement, no longer need a medication, or are concerned about the side effects of maintenance medicines for emotional and attention issues, it's worth talking to a doctor about your future without those prescriptions. No matter what, never stop taking a prescribed medication without discussing it with your doctor—you could be putting yourself at risk for uncomfortable or dangerous side effects, even if you've been taking very low doses and are feeling fine.

DAILY LIVING SKILLS

✔ **Develop a plan to ensure compliance.** Work with your parents on a plan to make sure you take your medication on time and meet any special dietary or environmental conditions. The best system might be one that worked for you in the past for something other than medication.

✔ **Set up reminder systems.** How will you remember to take medications or follow special medical routines? Would having an external alarm on a cell phone or buying a watch with multiple alarms help? Check out watchminder, which is made especially for individuals with ADHD—it vibrates and displays text messages—or purchase a regular sports watch. Any watch that has multiple alarms will do.

✔ **Check out online calendars, smartphone apps, or other technology** that can send email or text message reminders. Check out Google Calendar at http://www.google.com/googlecalendar/about.html. If you have a smartphone or iPad, find out what apps are available to help with remembering your medication.

✔ **Link new habits to old ones.** Think about how you can fit taking medication into a daily routine you already have. Taking your medications before you shower or after brushing your teeth might be a good way to remember. Would getting organized the night before school and making sure that medication is out and ready to go for the next day help?

Watchminder: **http://www.watchminder.com**.

Google Calendar: **http://www.google.com/googlecalendar/about.html**

RxmindMe: **http://www.rxmind.me/Default.aspx**

DAILY LIVING SKILLS

Making Appointments and
Calling for Prescription Refills

Part of being responsible for managing your health is being able to schedule appointments and order prescription refills. Calling the campus health center to schedule an appointment can be daunting if you've never done it before, especially if you're already sick and feeling low on energy. Taking over these new responsibilities while you're adjusting to so many other things, like learning to request your own accommodations, getting along with your roommate, and staying on top of rigorous academics, can make responsibilities that seem simple (like calling the doctor) feel enormous. If you can assume some of these responsibilities before taking off for college, it'll make the other adjustments go more smoothly.

✓ **Create several lists.** Make a list of your doctors and their phone numbers, as well as the names and dosages of any medication you take. It's a good idea to record this information in several places—your cell phone, computer files, and paper files, for example.

✓ **Check out your medical insurance.** Make sure that you have all the necessary insurance information—insurer's name, policy numbers, forms for medication, and an insurance card are big ones. Ask questions. Are you still covered on your parents' policy? How does your medical insurance work for appointments and prescriptions? What the heck is a co-pay? Do you have one? If so, how much?

✓ **Set up a system for getting refills or making appointments for check-ups.** Think about what tools you will use to remind yourself to order medications. Some teens count out the days new prescriptions will last and program their cell phone to provide a reminder about a week before they will run out of their medications. Some mail-order pharmacies will call or email you to remind you when your medication needs refilling, and they can also be less expensive. Would either plan work for you? What about calling for appointments? Using online calendars, cell phones, and other external reminders can help you to remember. Don't be afraid to set multiple reminders for the same thing if you're likely to hit "ignore" on your phone.

✔ **Set a cut-off date.** Come to an agreement with your parents about when they will no longer be involved in helping you order medications or call doctors.

✔ **Practice.** Taking responsibility for making other non-essential appointments, like haircuts, can be a good way to practice for the more important phone calls.

Preparing Meals and Choosing Healthy Foods

At college you will be totally in charge of what you eat, with no one looking over your shoulder. As a result, many college students, especially those with unlimited food plans, go a little wild and eat more than they had in the past or order food for take-out late into the night, making many unhealthy food choices. Most freshmen even expect to gain weight during this transition.

From our work with teens with ADHD/LD, we have observed that the stress of organization and time management can be even greater for them, and that can make the struggle to eat well in college even harder for you than for your non-ADHD/LD classmates. We have met some teens who do not make time for meals when their lives become too stressful and others whose medications may cause them to skip meals and who end up binging later at night on pizza and junk food when their medication wears off and they become hungry.

It's great that you have identified this as one skill that needs to be a part of your personalized training process. The following information will hopefully be helpful as you begin to build skills.

✔ **Learn all you can about healthy eating.** You might begin by searching the internet for tips on healthy eating for teens or avoiding weight gain in college. Before you can eat or prepare healthy meals, you'll need to know what types and amounts of food are suggested for young adults your age to eat in a day. Your primary care doctor can be a great resource for healthy eating ideas or for a referral to a nutritionist.

DAILY LIVING SKILLS

✔ **Look up dietary requirements for people with ADHD/LD.** Specific dietary guidelines have been suggested for individuals with ADHD/LD. In their recent book, **Delivered from Distraction,** Drs. Edward Hallowell and John Ratey summarize the latest research on what foods might be helpful to the brain. They specifically write about the importance of having a diet that is rich in omega-3 fatty acids—contained in salmon, sardines, tuna, and flaxseeds—to help the brain create chemicals that improve attention.

✔ **Look for resources in your community.** Does your school offer a health class with sessions on healthy eating and meal preparation? Can the school nurse offer any additional information on these topics? What about your medical doctor? There might be courses at local hospitals. Is there an older brother or sister or cousin who might play the role of a healthy-eating mentor? Are there any cooking classes geared to teens in your community?

✔ **Practice!** Work with a parent or older sibling to create a menu for a week and practice shopping and preparing meals together. Assume responsibility for your breakfast and lunch every day and try to make good choices for snacks.

✔ **Get in the habit of eating regularly.** Avoid skipping meals or going too long without eating. Set reminders on a phone or watch if this is a problem for you.

✔ **Deal with more serious eating or weight problems now.** If you have more significant eating issues like binge eating, purging (bulimia), or anorexia, now is the time to get more help. Facing more significant eating issues now will hopefully help you avoid greater problems later. If you already have a weight problem, do some research at school or online to learn about various supports like Overeaters Anonymous or Weight Watchers.

DAILY LIVING SKILLS

Beat the Freshman 15: **http://www.ecampustours.com/campuslife/ yourfreshmanyear/beatthefreshman15.htm.**

Food and Fitness: **http://kidshealth.org/teen/food_fitness.**

Tablespoons & Teaspoons: Teaching Teens With LD the Art of Meal Preparation: **http://www.greatschools.org/LD/school-learning/ tablespoons-and-teaspoons-teachingteens-with-ld-the-art- of-meal-preparation.gs?content=926**

Litt, A. S. (2005). *The college student's guide to eating well on campus.* Bethesda, MD: Tulip Hill Press.

Smith, M. J. (2006).*The smart student's guide to healthy living: How to survive stress, late nights, and the college cafeteria.* Oakland, CA: New Harbinger Publications.

Hallowell, E., & Ratey, J. (2006) *Delivered from distraction: Getting the most out of life with Attention Deficit Disorder.* New York, NY: Ballantine Books.

Fooducate: **http://www.fooducate.com**. This free iPhone app allows you to scan a barcode at the grocery store; it'll provide you with in-depth nutrition and health information about that product. They also have a blog and Twitter feed. You might not do much grocery shopping in college if you live on campus or subscribe to a meal plan, but if you use this app at home before you go to school, you'll have a better understanding of what types of foods contain what kind of health benefits by the time you're facing the dining hall.

Sparkrecipies: **http://www.sparkrecipes.com.** This healthy recipes site also has smartphone apps and features tons of search options.

Getting Adequate Exercise

Getting adequate exercise to maintain or lose weight and to balance stress is another important skill in the area of self-care for all teens and adults. Exercise is even more critical if you have been diagnosed with learning, attention, and emotional challenges. There is ample evidence that daily aerobic activity can have significant impact on the brains of individuals in general as well as those with specific difficulties. Exercise can improve overall attention and mood, and can lower stress levels and improve sleep. In his recent book, **Spark**, Dr. John Ratey states that exercise provides an unparalleled stimulus, creating an environment in which the brain is ready, willing, and able to learn.

Many teens with ADHD/LD diagnoses excel in sports and, thanks to the support of their parents, have been involved in team and individual sports as a way to channel their energy and to develop their talents. This involvement can mean regular exercise is built into your life because of practice, games, and meets. However, unless you're also recruited to college because of your athletic ability, you will most likely lose the external structure of playing a sport that you had in high school. That might seem like a small change, but it can result in difficulty with restlessness, sleep, attention, and stress. On the other hand, many teens have never had the opportunity to experience the positive role exercise can play on general well-being. If you are one of these teens, the following suggestions may help.

✔ **Learn about the benefits of exercise.** First, learn more about what exercise can do for you and your brain. Search the Internet for "exercise and the brain" or "exercise and ADHD and/or LD."

✔ **Set a realistic goal for exercise** and think through exercise activities that you feel are possible and that you might like. Be creative. If you hate to run, don't commit to hopping on the treadmill, but think about trying a dance class or learning to ski or swim.

✔ **Think about what would work** to make exercise more enjoyable and more likely to happen. When would it fit in your schedule? Put workouts on your calendar. Would joining a team or a gym help? Once accepted, find out if your college provides weekly exercise classes. Check out intramural sports teams that don't require tryouts. Would it help to have an exercise buddy?

DAILY LIVING SKILLS

✔ **Design a plan** for forming this new habit of regular exercise and build in regular check-ins to evaluate how things are going and what you are noticing on the days when you exercise and on the days you don't. Hopefully, you'll see the benefits of regular exercise and will be more motivated and committed to keeping to the plan.

✔ **Ask a parent, friend, or sibling for support in reaching your exercise goals.** You can decide how much support you want from the people around you by giving them permission to ask certain questions. For example, one teen gave her mom permission to ask, "I noticed that you skipped exercise today. Is that really what you want to do?" If you're in charge of telling your supporters what they can ask you, you'll be more likely to respond well to their questions.

✔ **Know when enough is enough.** For some, exercise can become addictive. The endorphins generated during vigorous workouts result in a natural high that some people crave. Others may use exercise to maintain or lose weight. If the amount of time you're devoting to exercise seems to be excessive and you're leaving little time for other activities, take a look at your motives and ask for help if you need to.

Runkeeper: **http://runkeeper.com**. An online community-based fitness tracker, which includes smartphone apps.

MapMyRide: **http://www.mapmyride.com**. Another online community, with a focus on using GPS tools to log runs, bike rides, hikes, and swims.

Ratey, J. (2008). *Spark: The revolutionary new science of exercise and the brain.* New York, NY: Little Brown and Company.

Managing Money

Problems in money management are commonplace for many college students (and for many adults as well!). It's all too easy to get into trouble in college if you lack money management skills—there are many temptations and you'll be spending money with no adult supervision. Plus, the cost of college has risen steadily in the last decade, so student loans, financial aid, and credit cards are a critical part of many students' lives. Understanding loans and credit is not a simple task for anyone, and it's increasingly necessary for college students to figure these things out on their own. If you already have trouble with organization or learning, it's a good idea to be as prepared as possible for dealing with these financial challenges that can reduce even the best-organized person to hair-pulling.

Use the tips below as you make your action plan for improving in this important skill.

✔ **Check out resources online and in your community.** Most banks have staff who will meet with customers to help with money management. Non-profit agencies in the community, as well as your place of worship or your local YMCA, may have workshops and courses, too. Many programs for women in the community provide free financial planning assistance. See what resources exist in your community, at your high school, and at the local community colleges.

✔ **Target your specific problems.** It might help to ask your parents if they can foresee any problems based on past issues you've had. They might notice that you have a hard time with money management based on unnecessary shopping trips or large telephone bills for texting. (Depending on your parents, you might already know all too well what they think you have trouble with!) Do you have a credit card? Who pays it off? If you do, do you pay on time and in full? If you've never talked to your parents about your money management, do it now. If it's a frequent argument, try to listen anew to what they have to say on this subject. Greater awareness can help you set goals to improve your skills.

✔ **Look for ways to earn more money.** Talk with your parents about doing chores or getting some part-time work. At college you'll have more free time to get a part-time job to earn spending money or discounts on clothes or books.

✓ **Open your own bank account** while you're still in high school to get familiar with tracking expenses. If you're going to be writing checks instead of using a debit or check card, you'll need to learn how to balance your checkbook or set up an online banking account. Be sure to make a habit of checking your online accounts a few times a week to make sure everything looks ok, or set up fraud alerts and low-balance warnings with your bank.

✓ **Think about what would work best for you—cash or credit cards.** Do you do better when using actual money, having a check book, or using an ATM card? Many of the students we worked with learned that it was better to work with cash and not use check cards as a way of life. If you have trouble with organization and thinking through actions, it can be easy to overspend when using plastic. Money is three dimensional and as it decreases in quantity and denomination, it's easier to see the consequences of monetary decisions. On the other hand, having a bunch of cash in your wallet can be tempting—it's already there, out of your bank account, ready to spend, so why not spend it? The more you know about how you relate to money, the better you'll be able to manage it.

✓ **Set up a budget.** There are many resources that will allow you to track expenses over a period of time so you become aware of where you're spending your money. Keep a log of how you spend your allowance or the money you make at work and try setting up a budget. Once you've recorded your expenses, you'll be able to see your habits and what needs to change. Would it help to use your cell phone or an online money budgeting program to track expenses?

✓ **Learn how to use a credit card.** Talk to your parents about how credit cards work (interest rates, minimum payments, late fees, etc.) and ask them to set up a card for you with a limited line of credit. If you both decide that you can be trusted with a credit card, it may make sense to try this skill during high school when they can oversee what happens.

✓ **Become knowledgeable about all of your financial obligations.** Given the expense of college today, many students need to take out student loans and grants. If you do take out a loan, make sure that you are familiar with your responsibilities and keep track of the amount of debt you will have to pay back after you graduate. Meet with the folks at the financial aid office once you are on campus. Know what you will have to do to get funds transferred to pay for tuition and other bills. Ask questions. When will you need to start making payments on these loans? What happens if you drop out for a time or are asked to leave? What if you can't find a job right away after graduation?

Sarkis, S. M., & Klein, K. (2009). *ADD and your money: A guide to personal finance for adults with Attention Deficit Disorder.* Oakland, CA: New Harbinger Publications.

Mint: **http://www.mint.com**. Mint is the be-all, end-all free personal finance tool. It's web-based and has smartphone apps. It can link directly to your bank account to track and categorize your expenses, create personal spending charts, and auto-calculate personalized, customizable budgets. They have really rigid privacy and security technology, too.

Making Good Decisions About Handling Daily Stress

Life and stress go hand in hand. The right amount of stress can enhance our lives, helping us perform better and take action when needed. And there are predictable times in life, often when we're dealing with changes, when stress can't be avoided. The real problems occur when we experience chronic stress or too much stress at one time. When this happens, if we don't have the right tools, things can get out of control, our learning and behavior can be hampered, and our bodies can't cope. High school can be an especially stressful time for teens because of your age; the normal adolescent issues you're facing; and the pressure to fit in, look good, and do well in school. It also stands to reason that all college-bound teens, even those without any learning, attention, and/or emotional disabilities, will encounter additional stress as they adapt to their new world with its greater responsibilities. Researchers studying college students report that many teens experience mental-health and stress-related problems during this transition time and have to seek help (Kadison, 2004). The good news is that sometimes you can prevent stress, and even when you can't, you can learn how to manage stress more effectively. Here are some ideas to use if you need to work on this college readiness skill.

✔ **Look at your pattern for handling stress.** Think about times when you handled things quite well and when things didn't go so well. How did not managing stress well affect your decisions, learning, behavior, and life in general? Ask your parents for feedback about what they have noticed.

✔ **Make a list of what helps.** What have you learned helps you during stressful times?

✔ **Look for problem responses.** If you are having extreme difficulties coping with stress or are using non-productive coping mechanisms like eating, drugs, or alcohol, look for help in your community. Now is the time to deal with these serious problems.

✔ **Learn about more productive ways to handle stress.** Conduct an Internet search on the topic of teens and stress or handling the stress of college. There are thousands of great websites targeted to helping teens handle stress.

✔ **Take care of yourself and your body every day.** This can help you be more resilient when going through highly stressful times. Having a healthy, balanced daily life with work and play, rest, food, exercise, and downtime can help create a buffer against the times that are tough to bear.

✔ **Plan ahead to prevent stress.** Do regular, big picture (weekly, monthly, semester) planning and mark a monthly calendar to spot the really busy times ahead. Planners that only show a day at a time or a week spread out over several pages don't give the same visual wake-up call that a monthly or quarterly calendar does. Schedule big school assignments and big social or sporting events on this big picture calendar to clearly see the weeks that will be really stressful. By seeing these hectic times in advance, it is possible to be proactive and avoid being overwhelmed.

✔ **Don't give up, ask for help.** When stress hits, as it inevitably does, don't let go of the daily activities that keep you well. Don't ignore the warning signs of stress, but instead practice noticing the feelings you are having and ask why you are having them. Reach out to others for support: This is the time to talk to friends and family and ask who the resource people are that can help.

✔ **Do the things that you know will calm you**—breathe, listen to music, exercise, pet your dog, meditate, or do anything else you know helps. This is really important and can do so much to help you stay focused even when times are tough.

✔ **Problem-solve to decrease the stress.** Identify the problem. Trust that there is a solution to the problem. Brainstorm options. Pick the one that you think is best. Break the problem into manageable parts. Take action!

ORGANIZATION

Organizing Your Room and Possessions

Most teens have rooms that look chaotic at times, but, for a number of reasons, having a room that is totally out of control or disorganized may be more common for some teens diagnosed with ADHD/LD. First of all, the same executive functioning skills we've talked about before—the ones that are at the root of learning, attention, and self-control problems—are also at the heart of the difficulties keeping things in order. In addition, if you have ADHD/LD, you might be so bogged down with outside activities to fix academic problems that you don't

DAILY LIVING SKILLS

have time to focus on these daily life priorities. Tutoring, seeing thera-pists, and talking with coaches can take up valuable time and energy that you could otherwise devote to putting away or even alphabetizing your DVD collection. Plus, there are all the normal activities and the treadmill of teenage life that can keep you from having time to develop a routine to clean your room and organize your stuff.

You can probably guess that college roommates won't love you like your parents do and they might be less able or willing to ignore the devastation on the other side of the room, suite, or apartment. Here are some tips on building this skill.

Some teens have become resistant to dealing with keeping their room clean because of their parents' constant pressure and nagging. Even if they do know how to clean their room, they do not slow down and take the time to get it done. Others who had a parent director or a parent repairman who filled the gaps (see discussion of these parent types on pages 13–14) may never have had to learn this important daily living skill. Now is the time to talk with your parents about why you need to work on daily living skills. Enlist their help, but don't fall back into letting them take over for you.

✔ **Think about the possible causes** for the disorganization in your room and with possessions. For example: Maybe you've developed a habit of dropping things on the floor, on a dining room table, or anywhere you might be, rather than taking the moment to put the item in a specific location. Having a mind that is on fast-forward or is not fully focused can lead teens with ADHD/LD to develop this habit. Other teens acknowledge and care about the problem, but it seems too big to tackle so they just keep adding to the mess because they find it hard to think through or figure out a plan of attack.

✔ **Establish a definition of a clean room.** Talk with your parents and come up with an agreed-upon definition of what a "clean" room looks like. Ask yourself what a clean room really needs to look like and why it's helpful to daily life.

✔ **Draw up a two-part plan.** Most teens will need a two-part plan—one to impose order on the mess that currently exists and another to keep that order going. Think more about your definition or dream of what a clean room would look like, and then think about what steps you'll need to take to turn this dream into reality. This step can involve a lot of emotions, particularly frustration. Instead of using your thoughts to come up with a plan, your emotional reactions to how huge the mess is and not knowing where to start may block your ability to turn on your problem-solving skills. It's also easy to get so lost trying to think of the perfect plan and perfect way to clean a room that you never take the first step. Think about how to get started with small steps that you can take each day; don't wait until the weekend or a vacation when a perfect cleaning plan can begin.

✔ **Make a list of the supplies or materials** that you may need to get started: garbage bags for trash or old clothes, boxes, plastic tubs or containers to keep things in, cleaning supplies, etc. Your parents can help you complete this list.

✔ **Put it on your schedule.** Grounding the plan in time is the key to making it happen. Time is available during the week, even if it's only 10–15 minutes. How about your time during the weekend?

✔ **Talk it out.** If you get stuck, get some additional ideas. Ask your friends how they go about cleaning their rooms, or ask an older sibling or cousin for help. Some tasks like this are easier with a buddy, for young people and adults alike.

✔ **Decide how you will attack the task.** For example: Do you want to start by category or by location? If you're cleaning by category you might find all the clean clothes and put those away, then all the dirty clothes, then school stuff, CDs, and video games. If you're cleaning by location, clear off the bed, then the desk, then the floor, and so on.

✔ **Finally, think about how you will keep order in the room once it is clean.** Try to set up a daily time to straighten things rather than a weekly or monthly big clean up. The goal is for you to learn to slow down and prevent a mess rather than live in the all-or-nothing pattern that led to the chaos in the room in the first place.

Keeping Track of Possessions

Problems in this skill tend to go hand-in-hand with problems keeping your room in order. If possessions like keys, wallets, cell phones, CDs, homework assignments, school books, sports equipment (the list goes on and on) don't have a predictable home, they can get lost, temporarily or forever. Life can get rocky in college if you never know where your dorm access card is, so here are some tips.

This common problem can turn your parents into chronic enablers, and they might take over reminding, nagging, and picking things up, all in an attempt to prevent the reoccurring catastrophes of misplaced objects. If your parent is part of the problem, you will all need to have an honest talk about how important it is that they change so you can learn now before you are on your own.

✔ **Analyze the situation.** Ask yourself about how and why this chronic problem happens. Make a list of things you tend to lose, times you tend to lose them, and things you never have a problem finding.

✔ **Figure out what has worked.** Think of some possession that you have been able to keep track of or a time when you seemed better able to keep track of things. The possible strategies for improving this skill are tucked away in the examples of success that you can recall. Make a list.

✔ **Collect ideas from friends or from your family.** We've said this before, but other people can act like mirrors and help you see aspects of yourself that you might not be able to see on your own. Plus, friends and family may have struggled with similar problems, and might have useful ideas for improving the situation.

✓ **Create a home for the possession that keeps getting lost.** Select a specific location in a space that makes sense to you. Would a basket by the door work? Or a shelf in your room? Be creative. If you need to park your keys, phone, and wallet in the bathroom, go for it!

✓ **Create reminders.** Will you need reminders to remember to use the new home or parking lot? What about having a reminder programmed into your cell phone that goes off at a logical time and asks, "Where is your stuff?" You can use a Google calendar to send multiple reminders during the day asking, "Do you know where your ____ is?"

✓ **Investigate technology that might help when things are lost.** There are products you can use to find things like keys, remotes, and cell phones. http://www.keyringer.com or http://www.findonefindall.com are two examples.

TIME MANAGEMENT

Getting Up and Out the Door in the Morning

Many teenagers don't get to bed at a reasonable time, don't get enough sleep, and have difficulty getting up the next morning. If you're one of them, you may also have allowed your parents to act as your human alarm clock. If you're a deep sleeper or fall asleep just a few hours before it's time to get up, you may not hear even the loudest alarm. It might take a parent bellowing, pulling back the covers or—if they are courageous—shaking you, to get you out of bed.

If you haven't learned how to fall asleep and wake up independently before going to college, you risk missing classes or even sleeping through exams, which can affect your grades. More importantly, if you sleep better, you'll feel better, and who doesn't want that?

DAILY LIVING SKILLS

Ask your parents to support you as you try to master this skill. Explaining your reasons and why you want to get up on your own now will help. You may need to give them permission to let go and allow you to miss the bus or even to miss school on important days so that you can learn to face the consequences of the choices you made the night before. Making mistakes while you're still at home where your parents are around to help you process the reasons for what happened and assist you in making a new plan of action is a safer way for you to learn than when you are miles away at college.

Here are some tips to help you create an action plan to work on waking up independently.

✔ **Analyze the reasons.** Analyze why getting to sleep at a reasonable hour and waking up independently are problematic for you. Pinpointing your unique set of reasons is the first step in figuring out a personalized plan for improvement.

✔ **Find out what works.** Was it easier to wake up when there was something exciting going on at school or if a friend was driving that day? Identify what seems to help you get up more easily.

✔ **Plan ahead.** See what you can do the night before to make mornings go more smoothly. Selecting your clothes, making lunch, packing your backpack, and showering the night before are just a few ways you might save time in the morning.

✔ **Create a nighttime routine** that will help you relax and get to sleep. See suggestions for this tip in the skill below (page 85).

✔ **Find the ideal alarm.** Explore ideas for alarms that will do the job of waking you up. Would a clock radio set on a loud station work better than an alarm? How about several alarms staggered at different times and in different places in the room? A number of companies make extra-loud alarms. Some college students with extreme difficulty waking up have found that vibrating alarms for individuals who are deaf or have hearing loss are helpful.

Citrus Alarm Clock: **http://www.ornj.net/citrus**. This clock can set different alarms for different days, which is good for students with unpredictable schedules.

Clocky: **http://www.alarmclockonline.com/clocky.htm**. Clocky is a rolling alarm clock that rolls off furniture onto the floor and continues moving around until you get out of bed to turn it off.

Online Alarm Clock: **http://onlineclock.net**. This is pretty much what it sounds like: a Web-based alarm clock that you can access on any computer.

Getting to Bed at a Reasonable Time to Get Enough Sleep

In general, life for teenagers is at total odds with their sleep patterns. Most experts state that the biological clock for an adolescent gets pushed back later and later. However, your bodies still require 8.5 to 9.5 hours of sleep, and high schools start classes earlier in the morning for teens than for any other age group. So your body is telling you to stay up late, your school is telling you to get up early, and your brain is telling you that if you go to bed when your body wants and get up when your school wants, you're going to be seriously groggy.

The situation can be even worse for teens like you who are diagnosed with ADHD/LD. Many experts believe that the same brain-related differences that underlie these disabilities are related to sleep issues. Some teens diagnosed with these disabilities tend to be night owls and get in the habit of doing schoolwork when the house is quiet and then going to bed in the wee hours of the morning. Others have trouble quieting their thoughts or emotions and falling asleep even when their body is fatigued. Some teens with these differences wake up to turn over or go to the bathroom and find it next to impossible to get back to sleep.

Sound familiar? Don't panic. For one thing, you'll have more freedom to choose your schedule in college, and you can try to schedule classes that start later in the day to allow yourself to sleep in if you really do your best work at night. But even if you don't have to be up until noon each day, it's a good idea to learn and practice getting yourself to bed at a reasonable hour—you can't always schedule your classes exactly the way you want, and you might find you need as much time during the day as you can get to complete your work. Your sleep patterns are not out of your control; here are some tips to help you get to bed at a reasonable time.

✔ **Get an evaluation for a possible sleep disorder.** If you and your parents have wondered about the possibility of your having a real, full-blown sleep disorder, now is the time, before college, to check this out. Call your doctor and find out about sleep disorder experts in your community. Many local hospitals also have sleep study centers.

✔ **Analyze the reasons** why you aren't getting to sleep at a reasonable hour. Pinpointing your unique set of reasons is the first step in figuring out a plan for improvement.

✔ **Check out your caffeine intake and use of energy drinks.** These legal substances are popular and can be used in unhealthy quantities as a way to deal with busy times in life. Too much caffeine will definitely make it difficult to get to sleep at night!

✔ **Make sure you are taking your stimulant medication as prescribed.** Doctors frequently give specific orders not to take these medications past a certain time. We know teens who deliberately took their medication later in the evening or took more doses in the day to be able to handle busy social and academic schedules. If that sounds like you, have a meeting with your prescribing doctor for an honest talk. Some teens we know admitted to us that they were actually abusing their prescribed medication, causing them to have problems sleeping. It can be tempting to misuse stimulant medications, but now is the time to deal with this serious problem.

✔ **Think about times when going to sleep was easier.** Maybe sleep is better when you exercise, or when you are on top of school work and don't feel worried or anxious. Identify what seems to help you fall asleep more easily.

✔ **Determine your sleep needs.** How much sleep do you feel is adequate for you to feel alert and rested throughout the day? Learn the truth about how much sleep you really need to be at your best. All people need rest, but experts tell us that sleep may be even more important for people whose brains are wired differently and who have ADHD/LD.

✔ **Determine a time for lights out.** When would the lights need to go out for you to get the amount of sleep you identified above? What would need to happen earlier in the day or evening for you to be ready to turn the lights out at this time? Would it help to set the alarm on a cell phone to go off each night an hour before the time you identified?

✔ **Set up a nighttime routine.** Think about a nighttime routine that would help you unwind. When should you finish homework and studying? What about getting everything ready for the next day? Would it help to have some downtime, like reading or listening to music, right before lights out? Should you leave your cell phone somewhere other than in the bedroom so you won't be tempted to text your friends late into the night? Should you turn off your laptop? Many sleep researchers agree that it's a good idea to stop looking at backlit screens at least a half hour before lights out to help improve the quality of sleep, but some people are comforted by the sounds of a soft TV in the background. Bottom line: Know what works for you, and do it every night.

SleepCycle: **http://mdlabs.se/sleepcycle/index.html**.
This app uses the iPhone's accelerometer to monitor your movement while you sleep and create graphs of your sleep cycles.

DAILY LIVING SKILLS

Balancing Fun, Chores, and Schoolwork

As you are now well aware, the daily life of the college student is totally different than the daily life of a high school student, with much more unstructured time and opportunity for choice. College students spend fewer hours in class and there are different schedules for different days with larger open blocks of time during the week and evenings . . . not to mention the weekends. Time management problems will not go away in college and now is a great time to work on sticking to tasks and managing your time.

It can be tough to create your own structure and find the perfect balance between friends, school work, classes, chores, downtime, and time for eating and sleeping. But in our experience, getting this balance right may be more important for success in college than the grades you got in high school or your SAT scores.

The teens we talk to usually fall into two categories: mostly work, and mostly play. Some teens with ADHD/LD tell us that in high school they used the only learning strategy that they could count on—working harder (and usually longer). Other teens tell us that they were all play and did little to no work in high school and could get good grades by listening in class and glancing at their book the night before the exam. If either of these patterns sound familiar, try some of these tips.

✔ **Imagine a balanced schedule.** Ask yourself, "If I had a magic wand and could have the perfectly balanced day or week, what would the schedule look like?" What activities are excluded and/or included in this dream? Does the dream have more time to chill and do nothing? Does it have you getting work done earlier in the day or the week? Make a list of the key qualities that you described in this perfect scenario.

✔ **Develop a plan.** What would it take to make this dream a reality? Do some of your activities have to go to make more room for downtime, sleep, exercise, and social time? Or do you need to limit distracting time fillers like TV, surfing the web, visiting social networking sites, and playing video games? Do you need to use time differently during the day at school, in study hall, or in special resource support?

Talk with your parents about how they can gradually allow you to be in charge of designing your schedule. What role do you need them to play as you learn how to do this?

✔ **Create a master schedule.** Most experts on time management start with this same suggestion. Here's how to get started. First, make a weekly schedule that represents your life right now. Mark out classes, travel time to and from school, meals, sleep, sports, reoccurring meetings, appointments, etc. Then, look at the times you already have on your schedule. Find where the unstructured or open blocks of time really are and count up how much open time there really is. Sometimes, this visual of life speaks volumes about what needs to change and shows you how much time you're spending on activities that aren't of value to you, or that you are taking way too long to do school assignments that should be done more quickly.

Now the real work begins. First, decide what small steps you might take each day to make life more balanced. Do you need some downtime each day to do something that you love, like drawing, painting, playing an instrument, or exercising? Or are you too good at doing what you love and avoiding responsibilities? Maybe you need to come right home after school, avoid the TV or computer, and get right to doing school work on daily assignments and long-term assignments.

Next, have a look at the weekends. Should you take a break and do something fun on Friday and a little each day because you are overworking? Or should you decide to do your homework or the project that is the hardest on Friday afternoon to get it out of the way to avoid the Sunday-night nightmare when you can't avoid the hard work anymore?

Now make a new master schedule for the next week that is more balanced and moving in the direction of your dream and vision of a balanced life.

Freedom: **http://macfreedom.com**. Freedom prevents you from accessing the Internet for up to eight hours at a time and is a favorite of folks who write novels. It's available for all operating systems.

Vitamin R: **http://www.publicspace.net/Vitamin-R**. If the computer-installed Solitaire is a distraction for you, just blocking the internet won't do much good. Vitamin R can block software or downloaded applications that are problematic.

Self Control. **http://visitsteve.com/made/selfcontrol**. Self Control is a Mac-only application that will block your ability to go to specified websites for a period of time.

Getting Places on Time

Managing time can be particularly difficult with ADHD/LD. With the many competing demands for your time, it's easy to get off track and over-whelmed. In addition, research shows that it is difficult for many people with ADHD/LD to judge the passage of time. The first step in managing time, for you, might be realizing that you can't. Instead of focusing on getting things done in a certain time frame or arriving somewhere at a certain time, it might be better for you to just focus on getting the task done or getting where you need to be. Period. And without the pressure, you may find that you get better at setting up and sticking to a realistic plan to be on time.

The second most common reason for not being able to be on time seems to be over-commitment. Taking on one more task (e.g., putting in a load of laundry) or running another errand or stopping to check in with a friend can ruin the best designed plans, and then you find you're late again! The following are some steps you can take while working on this particular skill.

✔ **Identify what gets you off track.** Try to pinpoint what gets you off track in the first place. If you have a problem with the passage of time, wear a watch with an alarm or set up visual reminders (schedules) of what you should be doing and when. If you are distractible, use that to your advantage. Post visual reminders (e.g., signs, post-it notes, or screen savers) in your environment to keep you to a schedule or to remind yourself to stay on track.

✔ **Be accountable to someone else.** Call a friend or have a friend call you to check in and make sure you are working on what you should be doing or leaving when you need to in order to be on time. For many teens, having someone else involved provides the structure and accountability that they need to follow through with their plans.

✔ **Make a list.** If you tend to take on too many tasks in the morning, make a list and **stick to it!** Don't allow yourself to add one more thing!

The Procrastinator's Clock: **http://davidseah.com/2007/01/a-chindogu-clock-for-procrastinators**. This clock is either fast or on time, but it is not fast by a constant number of minutes, so you never know exactly how fast. Tricky!

Online "To Do" List: **http://www.teuxdeux.com**. TeuxDeux is a simple to-do app that has a free browser-based site as well as an iPhone app.

DAILY LIVING SKILLS

Academic Skills

Many students tell us that they had no clue how hard classes were going to be at a 4-year college. Typically, students (with and without diagnosed disabilities) discover that they need to develop new skills and to refine the skills they bring from high school to college. In this section, we offer tips and suggestions to make studying easier and to help you work on specific areas such as note-taking and reading for information.

SELF-KNOWLEDGE

Of all the classes you'll be taking in your first semester at college, the most important crash-course might be one that's not in your class catalog: Learning how you, personally, learn. Knowing your own preferences and problems will make you a more efficient student and can help you minimize stress or frustration in your classes.

Knowing Your Learning Style

Not all people learn the same way. You can find a lot of information and research about different learning styles. While some experts have questioned whether learning style differences really exist, other experts suggest our styles are unique and that matching teaching and learning activities to your own style can make learning easier. Regardless of what the experts say, many of the teens we know tell us that they wish they had fully understood how they best learned and studied before coming to college. Instead, many say they spent their first semester using trial and error while preparing for their first exams to figure out their style.

Use the questions and ideas below to think about your learning style and preferences.

✔ **Notice and see if you have a preference for how you like to learn new information.** If you prefer a more visual approach to learning, you might remember information better if there are pictures, diagrams, graphs, or charts. If you prefer auditory learning, you might remember information best if you hear it spoken, or you might like to have things explained or use audio books. If you like to be more active when learning new information by talking about what you learned, reteaching it, studying with others, demonstrating it, and drawing or writing information, you might be a more kinesthetic, activity-oriented learner.

✔ **Go over your psychoeducational evaluation** with your parents or meet with the person who did the evaluation and look for hints about what your preferred learning style might be.

✔ **Think about what worked.** How did you study for a quiz or a test that went well? Think of a recent time when you did poorly on a paper or a quiz. How did you study and what might have worked better?

✔ **Do an online search** for "learning styles" and play around with some of the learning style quizzes that you find.

✔ **Interview some friends.** Gather ideas about the different ways they study. Try out some of these approaches and then evaluate how well (or not!) they worked for you.

✔ **Keep a journal** describing study strategies and evaluating how different techniques worked.

Going to College: **http://www.going-to-college.org**. In addition to lessons and activities, this site contains videos; links to learning-style surveys; and materials that students, teachers, and parents can use while preparing for and transitioning to college.

Knowing When and Where You Study Best

College will offer many options for studying that you have not experienced in high school. With no adults around, you can choose to study late into the night, well past the time when your parents would have forced you turn the lights out. Friends will invite you study at coffee shops, in study groups, in the lounge in their dorms, and in a host of other tempting environments. If you don't really know what time of day and what environment works best for you, or when it is time to change where and when you are studying, high school is the perfect time to find out.

To develop a plan for this skill, use some or all of the following techniques to gather information on when and where to study.

✔ **Reflect back** on successful and unsuccessful study sessions.

✔ **Analyze these sessions and create a journal.** Think about whether the study environment or time of day used for studying was a key factor in whether the study session paid off or not.

✔ **Make a list of all the possible study environments** available and rate them as to whether this setting might be helpful for studying.

✔ **Make a master schedule** of your day and identify when there are open times at school or at home for studying and doing school work.

ACADEMIC SKILLS

✔ **Rate each block.** How productive would this period of time be for studying and homework? Some students really are night owls who have their peak attention after dinner. Others need to use the mornings or afternoons to do the harder work, because their peak attention happens earlier in the day.

Getting Motivated to Face Difficult Assignments

Researchers say that the ability to keep working, even when an assignment is not very motivating, is an important quality found in successful college students. This ability is probably very important for success in life as well. How often in a day do you face tasks that you aren't thrilled to do, whether the task is at school or some chore at home? How do you motivate yourself to deal with a less-than-exciting or very difficult task?

Try some of the following suggestions to develop a plan to work on this skill.

✔ **Identify the types of tasks that you find most challenging** and talk with a parent, teacher, or friend about why you might be having problems with these particular tasks. Consider whether these tasks are directly rubbing up against your diagnosed disability. For example, you may tend to put off your reading assignments because sitting still for long periods is hard for you. Or if you have a learning disability in math, you might put off or skip your Algebra homework.

✔ **Identify patterns.** Keep a journal and record observations about what types of tasks you find challenging and what you were feeling when you tried to complete these tasks. Look for patterns. Were the tasks all in one subject area or of a similar type? Were problems related to not understanding or not reading directions? Not having adequate notes from class? Being too tired? Being in the wrong study environment? These are just examples—what other reasons have you discovered?

✔ **Try a new plan of action.** For example: Go to tutoring or study hall to work on homework. That way, if you run into difficulty, a teacher will be nearby to help. Set a time limit on how long you will try working on a problematic task before taking a break or calling a friend for help. Change things up a bit and see what helps.

✔ **Find all the resources available** at school or online for completing tasks that are challenging.

✔ **Think motivating thoughts** or create motivating incentives. For example, one teen we knew had a very difficult time with foreign languages. Knowing that taking this class was necessary for a college degree, she wrote herself a note that said, "This class will help you graduate and reach your dreams." This positive thought replaced her negative thought, "I hate memorizing Spanish vocabulary words."

✔ **Make doing the task more fun.** One student chose to do his least favorite tasks at a bookstore where he could sit in a cushy chair and sip on a flavored coffee. Another gave herself a reward of 10 minutes on Facebook for every 50 minutes she worked on a paper she found challenging. Another asked his roommate to wait to go to the gym so he could go along after he did his boring studying for Spanish class.

STUDY SKILLS

High school has taught you a lot of things, but it might not have taught you how to study. If that's the case, you don't want to wait until your first college midterms to learn that spending hours recopying notes might work for your roommate but isn't your own best use of valuable study time. Fortunately, there are plenty of tips and resources out there to help you develop the skills you need.

Walter, T. L., Siebert, A., & Smith, L. N. (2000). *Student success: How to succeed in college and still have time for your friends.* Orlando, FL: Harcourt Brace & Company.

Nist, S. L. & Holschuh, J. P. (2000). *Active learning: Strategies for college success.* Needham Heights, MA: Allyn & Bacon.

Paulk, W., & Owens, R. J. Q. (2007). *How to study in college,* 10th edition. Boston, MA: Houghton Mifflin. Free download: **http://the-manuals.com/how-to-study-in-college-walter-paulk-manual**.

Strichart, S.S., & Magrum II, C. T. (2002). *Teaching learning strategies and study skills to students with learning disabilities, attention deficit disorders or special needs,* 3rd edition. Needham Heights, MA: Allyn and Bacon.

Academic Success Videos from Dartmouth College. **http://www.dartmouth.edu/~acskills/videos/index.html**. There is one for every important college study skill.

The Learning Center. **http://learningcenter.unc.edu**. This site has handouts and animated videos about common college study skills.

Taking Notes From Reading Assignments

Many teens tell us that they did very well in high school without having to take notes from reading assignments because the details of what they read were discussed in class. In college, professors typically won't review all readings in-depth in class, yet questions from these assignments might be included on their exams. As a result, you're going to have to figure out what is important in the readings and how to keep track of important information, and taking notes from the readings is crucial.

To improve your note-taking skills during reading, try some or all of the following:

✔ **Look for a note-taking skills class.** Find out if there is a reading or study skills class available through your high school or at a nearby community college.

✓ **Find help.** Is there a special education teacher or a guidance counselor in your high school who has expertise in note-taking techniques who could meet with you to work on this skill?

✓ **Learn new methods.** Check out the school library and see what books might be available about effective skills for taking notes from reading assignments. A very popular technique is the SQRW method (see http://www. education.com/reference/article/SQRW-reading-taking-notes-textbooks). This method allows you to use the titles, subtitles, and visual materials in the text to figure out the purpose of a reading assignment and to come up with some questions that can guide your reading and note taking.

✓ **Look at a video.** Conduct a search on YouTube and check out the hundreds of videos on taking notes while reading.

Mooney, J., & Cole, D. (2000). *Learning outside the lines.* New York, NY: Fireside.

SQRW method: **http://www.education.com/reference/article/SQRW-reading-taking-notes-textbooks.**

Taking Notes That Are Complete and Useful

Most first-year college students we know have limited experience taking notes and learning in lecture classes. Given the smaller class size in high school, you might be most comfortable with learning in a discussion-oriented setting. However, many classes at large 4-year colleges consist of lecture classes of 50 to 100 students in which the professor talks for most of the class period with little or no time available for discussion or questions and answers.

It can be really challenging to learn and to take notes in this more passive learning environment. For some students with ADHD/LD, the struggle is very basic—they have trouble just sitting still and remaining attentive when there is no interaction. Others find professors' language and vocabulary unfamiliar, so they struggle with meaning and have to decipher what the professor is saying. Many students, even those without learning and attention challenges, struggle as they attempt to write down the key points being covered. To improve this skill, try the following:

- **Identify all the resources available at school** for learning more about taking complete notes in lecture classes. The guidance counselor, transition specialist, special education teacher, and librarian are good places to start.

- **Be prepared.** Taking notes begins before you even get to class and continues after class. This includes reviewing the notes and readings from the day before and checking the syllabus to become familiar with what the professor will discuss. Going to class familiar with the day's vocabulary and key concepts can make listening easier. Having a list of questions can also guide listening. This can make you, the listener, more focused as well.

- **Decide on a format for recording notes.** Once again, your preference should guide you. Will a linear system of taking notes using a traditional outline really work? Or do you do better with bullet points and indentations to separate main ideas from details? Some note-taking systems, like the Cornell Method, suggest making two columns, the left for the main points or key questions guiding the lecture and right for explanations. Most systems discourage students from writing full sentences or recording every word; instead, they suggest skipping filler words like "and" or "the" and focusing on key words and phrases. Most resources suggest that you spend some time soon after taking notes to summarize what the key points of the lecture were and to make a list of any questions that you might have.

- **Talk to your teacher.** Going to talk to the teacher in a one-on-one setting to review questions you have about the day's class can be good practice for how you will interact with professors or teaching assistants in college. Not all college courses allow for in-class questions, so you'll have to get used to going to office hours or study sessions and asking questions there.

- **Access accommodations.** For some students, learning and attention disabilities make note-taking nearly impossible. You might need to use available technologies and accommodations. Find out about the latest devices by checking with your county's Vocational Rehabilitation Assistive Technology Center, a special education teacher, or a transition specialist. Would you benefit from asking permission to use a digital tape recorder to supplement or take the place of written notes? Would you do better if you typed notes on a laptop? This might actually be good preparation, because many colleges allow or even require students to bring laptops to class. Would you benefit by having a copy of the teacher's notes or a classmate's notes as an accommodation? Some students find this accommodation critical since they cannot listen, remember, and write legibly.

✓ **Use technology.** Check out the latest note-taking technology, like the Pulse Smart Pen made by Livescribe (http://www.livescribe.com). This relatively inexpensive pen records the lecture as you write, so you don't have to worry about missing key details; you can go back later and tap the pen at the point on the page when you lost the lecture and the pen will play back the words that were spoken. With this pen, and with other digital recorders, you can download the audio version of the lecture and listen to it over again. Microsoft also includes OneNote in its Office suite. OneNote works like the smart pen, only instead of writing your notes you can type them on a laptop while recording the lecture. You can also find notetaking apps for smartphones.

Pulse Smart Pen: **http://www.livescribe.com/en-us.**

Microsoft OneNote: **http://office.microsoft.com/en-us/onenote.**

Digital Recorders: **http://www.planetheadset.com/usbmicrophone. php?gclid=CMqj_bCMmaQCFZJ17Aod_mi5Dw.**

Evernote: **http://www.evernote.com.** Evernote allows you to type notes, but it also recognizes handwriting from scanned notes and will save websites and photos. It has extensive organization capabilities, and it indexes your notes to make them searchable.

ACADEMIC SKILLS

Identifying What's Important While Reading

Reading a textbook or a novel that has been assigned for school can be overwhelming, especially if you haven't trained yourself to sort out what is important from what is not. While this may not be a skill that you needed much during high school, it is critical in college, where professors can assign hundreds of pages of reading a week and require several textbooks for one class.

The following suggestions will help you develop a plan to work on this important skill.

✔ **Look for audio options.** Would hearing the book on tape or having it read by text-reading software allow you to better comprehend what is important? Audio books are available for some assignments. Text recognition software allows a computerized voice to read an electronic file of a book or reading assignment. Check out companies that provide these audio options. There are also some organizations listed in the Books and Bookmarks section below that provide audio versions of text for individuals with vision and reading disabilities. Check these out to see if you qualify for their services. Some new ebook technologies have audio versions of etext, and if you have a smartphone, it may have an app that will provide an audio version of etexts.

✔ **Take careful notes.** Use the SQRW method for note-taking. See page 98 or visit **http://www.education.com/reference/article/SQRW-reading-taking-notes-textbooks**. The Survey step, which happens before reading, helps you identify what is important by looking at titles; subtitles; headings; visuals like pictures, tables, and graphs; and chapter summaries. From there, you can come up with questions (Q is step 2) that guide reading.

✔ **Look for clues.** Get in the habit of using the structure of the book to provide clues about the main concepts. When reading textbooks, be sure to look at the table of contents. The headings for sections can be used to sort out the important concepts from the lesser concepts and see how the ideas fit together.

✔ **Survey other class materials** for clues about what is important in the reading assignment. For example, check the syllabus to see if there are any objectives written for the class or the specific lecture for which the readings are assigned. Is there a study guide? Are there questions at the end of the chapter that will provide a hint about what the key information is?

✔ **Ask the teacher.** If the book, the syllabus, and the class notes don't provide any clues, meet with your teacher and ask for advice on what his or her expectations are for the reading assignments.

✔ **Monitor progress.** Keep a chart of test grades and quizzes before working on this skill, then compare your grades after you have been working for a while.

Recordings for the Blind and Dyslexic: **http://www.rfbd.org.** RFB&D is a national nonprofit organization that provides audio books to eligible students with disabilities.

Bookshare: **http://www.bookshare.org.** Bookshare offers digital books, textbooks, teacher-recommended reading, periodicals, and assistive technology tools to U.S. students with qualifying disabilities.

The following sites offer text reading software.
Natural Reader: **http://www.naturalreaders.com/?gclid=C MW04KWIsaACFYha2god5BxETA.**
Read & Write Gold: **http://www.texthelp.com/page.asp.**
Read Please: **http://www.readplease.com.**

These sites can convert text to audio files that you can save and play back later.
Zamzar: **http://www.zamzar.com.**
VozMe: **http://vozme.com.**

Organizing Ideas and Writing and Editing Papers

At a 4-year college, you'll face multiple writing assignments that may be more complex and longer than anything you've faced in high school. Sometimes, several papers are due during the same week of the semester. Unlike in high school, where teachers often break things into several smaller writing assignments, which are part of working on a larger paper, in college you'll be on your own. Facing these new expectations can be overwhelming if your disability interferes with any aspect of the writing process, especially if you're used to having help from parents and teachers who won't be available at college.

Some students depend on receiving extensions as a way to cope with writing difficulties. Others ask parents, relatives, friends, or teachers to read and help edit their papers. Because assignments tend to be less complex in high school, many students have learned to wait until the deadline and to write one draft of a paper. Even if these patterns have been rewarded with good grades in high school, you already know that college is different, and that extensions and guided help from the professors are less likely to be safety nets for you.

There is a lot of help for writing in college. The following suggestions may help you develop this skill.

✔ **Analyze the process.** Think about what part of the writing process is hardest for you, and why. If you've worked on papers in steps during high school, talk to the teacher who assigned the paper and ask which step was the weakest. Talk to your friends about their writing processes, too; you might find that there are steps or things you struggle with or do well at that you'd never thought about.

✔ **Identify patterns.** Look at old papers and identify patterns in teacher feedback. Talk to the teacher if anything is unclear, or if it looks like you're not making the kind of progress you want to make before college.

✔ **Analyze your approach to writing papers.** Do you think about writing as a process that happens over time or are you used to writing a final product close to the deadline?

✔ **Identify all the resources** available at school to help you work on writing.

✔ **Think more about your learning style** and how this knowledge can be applied to writing. What process would help you to organize and clarify ideas for a paper? Would talking the ideas through with the teacher or a friend help? Would taping the ideas be helpful before actually typing or writing them on the page? Maybe using a mind map or mind-mapping software can help you generate ideas and then organize them together. Do outlines really help? Would it work if you made a PowerPoint of your paper and talked out your ideas and then typed up what you said? Would speech-to-text software make writing easier so you could talk and let the computer type what you said? You can then edit what you dictated, either by hand or by voice.

✔ **Develop a proofreading process.** If proofreading is challenging for you, develop a proofreading process. Some general tips for proofreading suggest that you: Take a break after writing before proofreading a paper. Read the paper out loud to hear errors and other problems, like awkward passages or confusing structure. Consider using text-to-speech software to read the paper back out loud to you. When proofreading a paper on the computer, make the font very large and double-space the text. Collapse the window so only a line or two of text shows up at a time. Use the high-lighting feature to mark errors or sections of the paper that need to be reworked, rather than immediately making revisions. That way the proof-reading step is separated from the writing step. Create a personalized proofreading checklist based on your unique error patterns and keep it handy when you are proofing your papers.

✔ **Research your college.** A lot of colleges have writing centers that will help you with any paper at any point in the writing process, even if you just need someone to bounce ideas off before you've written a word. At many colleges, writing center tutors must train for a semester or a year before they can start tutoring, and they can be a great resource for students who would like one-on-one help at any stage of the writing process. Some writing centers specialize in working with students with ADHD/LD. Writing center staff also tend to be well informed about school policies on plagia-rism and honor codes, and can help you navigate the sometimes-fuzzy line between cheating and getting the help you need.

ACADEMIC SKILLS

Dragon Naturally Speaking: **http://www.nuance.com/dragon/in-dex.htm**. This speech-to-text software allows you to talk out your thoughts—the computer will "type" what you say.

Inspiration Software: **http://www.inspiration.com**.

University of Chicago Writing Program: **http://writing-program .uchicago.edu/resources/collegewriting/index.htm**. The University of Chicago Writing Program's website has a terrific in-depth guide to college writing, and begins by highlighting differences between high school and college writing.

University of North Carolina at Chapel Hill Writing Center: **http:// www.unc.edu/depts/wcweb/handouts/index.html**. This website has tons of handouts on different aspects of writing and has some animated videos that demonstrate aspects of the writing process.

Preparing for Tests and Exams

Many high school students, even those without disabilities, think they are very good at preparing for tests and exams and are totally shocked to realize that their test preparation methods might not get them the grades they want in college. In high school, tests tend to occur more frequently and cover smaller amounts of information; they may also emphasize memorizing information. However, exams in college are less frequent and require students to apply the factual knowledge they are learning and to think critically. Critical thinking is a more active process and requires the learner to analyze and synthesize information by putting it together to see relationships, similarities, and differences, and to form well-supported conclusions. Since many teens, not just those diagnosed with ADHD/LD, have limited experience with this type of thinking, they frequently are unprepared for the types of exams they face at college.

The following suggestions may help you work on your test prep skills.

✔ **Think about your strengths and weaknesses** when preparing for tests for different classes. When did you feel that you were well prepared? What strategies did you use? What worked and what didn't? What strategies helped you to prepare for different types of exams: multiple choice, short answer, and essay? For different subjects—History? Science? English? Math? What worked? What didn't work?

✔ **Start a file of strategies that work** for different classes and different test formats.

✔ **Identify all the resources** available in school and in the community for learning more about how to better prepare for tests and final exams. See what books are available in the school or community library.

✔ **Check out the Internet** for test preparation tips. We're including specific test-prep strategies here. Maybe some will work well for you:

+ Spread studying out over time, because it is not easy for anyone, even those without disabilities, to review and remember too much information in one sitting. Be sure you know what the test will cover and how the teacher will expect you to show what you know.

+ Start by studying the information that is less familiar and ending with the information that just needs to be reviewed. In case time runs short, studying the harder information first will pay off.

+ Make up questions as a way to test your knowledge for the exam.

+ Look at old exams and study guides and then create sample test questions.

+ Look at the back of textbooks for questions, especially questions that require you to apply or critically use the information.

+ Use the syllabus and course objectives to create a study guide and sample questions.

+ Practice the type of thinking that college tests will require and go beyond the fact level of who/what/when/where.

+ Practice comparing and contrasting information.

+ Practice describing and giving examples.

+ Practice identifying the significance of a person, event, or place. For science classes, practice explaining the function of an organ, comparing and contrasting different plants or animals, or describing the structure of an organ. For math and calculation-based classes, practice doing problems without opening the book.

+ Use your learning style to help you. If you tend to learn verbally, pretend to give a lecture on the topic. If you do best with visual learning, create charts, graphs, tables, timelines, and flow charts.

+ Practice answering the questions in the same way the test will demand it. If the test is an essay, practice writing an essay. At first the practice can be untimed and you can even allow yourself to refer back to notes, but eventually you should practice answering from memory. Recent studies suggest that recalling information from memory can improve test performance more than study periods where you're reviewing information or taking notes.

+ Think about the strategies to use when taking the actual exam. The test-taking process is as important as the study plan. Do an Internet search for test-taking strategies for different types of tests. Look at error patterns on old exams to figure out what went wrong. Did you miss questions because you didn't read carefully? Did you rush and not double-check your work? That can be frustrating, especially if you knew the answer but made a small error because you were moving too fast.

Headmagnet: **http://headmagnet.com**. Headmagnet is an online flashcard tool that uses research on memory, learning, and cognition to create smart quizzes. It has a social element, so you can learn with friends.

Study Stack: **http://www.studystack.com**. Another online flashcard tool, which allows you to create games and activities with your study lists.

Walter, T. L., Siebert, A., & Smith, L. N. (2000). *Student success: How to succeed in college and still have time for your friends.* Orlando, FL: Harcourt Brace & Company.

Nist, S. L., & Holschuh, J. (2000). *Active learning: Strategies for college success.* Needham Heights, MA: Allyn & Bacon.

Paulk, W., & Owens, R. J. Q. (2007). *How to study in college*, 10th edition. Boston, MA: Houghton Mifflin. Free download: **http://the-manuals.com/how-to-study-in-college-walter -paulk-manual**.

Strichart, S.S., & Magrum II, C. T. (2002). *Teaching learning strategies and study skills to students with learning disabilities, attention deficit disorders or special needs*, 3rd edition. Needham Heights, MA: Allyn & Bacon.

Belluck, P. (2011). "To really learn, quit studying and take a test." *New York Times*, retrieved on February 4, 20110 from **http://www .nytimes.com/2011/01/21/science/21memory.html**.

ACADEMIC SKILLS

Reviewing Class Notes and Assigned Readings on a Regular Basis

This is one skill that few first-year students have practiced, but it is critical to success in college. Most high schools have daily, graded homework and frequent quizzes and tests that serve to keep students up to date with work. Similarly, many students report that they have to participate in their smaller high school classes so, out of necessity, they stay on top of work. A lot of students really don't have any idea what to do when they are told to study, but in college, where there may be very little assigned, graded, outside-of-class work, you'll do better if you know how to study even when there aren't scheduled tests or papers. Because you've been diagnosed with ADHD/LD, you may find it especially difficult to act strategically in a crisis—like the crisis that comes from realizing you have considerable work to do to prepare for a test or complete a paper that is due soon. Stress, plus any difficulty you may have with self-management, can block you from problem-solving and finding a way to tackle the crisis. In addition, if you tend to work more slowly, crunch times can be especially challenging. Knowing how to study before deadlines and exam dates are looming will help you manage stressful times more efficiently. Here are some study tips to get you started.

✔ **Document progress.** Identify one or two classes in which your performance could be improved by studying regularly. Develop a table with your grades from previous tests and quizzes to compare to those taken after you begin studying more frequently.

✔ **Review.** Reread class notes and summarize the key concepts and ideas taught in the class.

✔ **Rehearse this information to commit it to memory.** Re-read assignments and class notes and create new, comprehensive notes that integrate the readings with the information you learned in class.

✔ **Create sample test questions** on this material and practice answering the questions, first with notes available and without worrying about time limits and then from total memory and with time as a factor.

✔ **Practice completing problems** when the subject is a calculation-based class.

✔ **Consult other sources** on the subject you're working on to study the information. Is there another book on the subject that you could read? What information is available on the Internet?

✔ **Use study techniques that match your learning style.** Would it be helpful to study with a friend and practice teaching one another? Would it help to tape-record a summary of the information you've studied? Would a written summary be better? What about creating a visual—like a flow chart, table, or graph—of the information you need to learn?

Study Rails: **http://www.studyrails.com/view/render_page**. Study Rails is an inexpensive assignment-management tool. You can track assignments, schedule time for completing things, block distracting sites or apps during your scheduled study time, and set up email or text reminders of due dates.

Using the Help Available in School

As you may have guessed by now, we feel that using the available resources to deal with an academic challenge is an important skill. For each of the study skills listed in this guide we have suggested that you identify all the available resources. Yet, we often see that this skill is under-developed in many college students, even those without disabilities. Too often, we witness students who feel that using a resource, like tutoring or learning-strategy instruction or even some new software, is a sign of weakness. Many of these students have been successful on their own by trying harder, or have sought help from family members without going to outside specialists. However, it's important to feel comfortable going to strangers to get the academic help you need.

ACADEMIC SKILLS

To help you to work on this skill during high school, try some or all of the following suggestions.

✓ **Research the specific academic help and emotional supports available at your high school.** Use the school website and talk to the guidance counselor or special class teacher to get a full picture of all the academic help available. You should also research the help available at the college you'll be attending before or immediately upon getting accepted. Don't wait until you get on campus and have too many other things to do.

✓ **Form a study group.** Talk with friends to see if any of them might be interested in forming a study group. This is what many successful college students do.

✓ **Go to help sessions prepared.** Make up a list of questions for the support-person you're talking to, and maybe even practice what to say ahead of time. Speaking up can be hard at first, especially if you are shy and new at getting help. You may want to have someone role-play this with you.

✓ **Take notes or tape the session.** If remembering what you talked about at the help session is a weakness for you, take notes or ask permission to tape the session using a digital recorder or the Livescribe pen.

TIME MANAGEMENT

You already know that your time in college will be less scheduled than your time in high school has been. To make the most of all the free time you're about to have, you'll need to learn how to manage your time.

Setting Up a Study Schedule

Granted, you may not have much flexibility in designing a study schedule, but it will be so helpful if you find a way to practice now. So, if you have acknowledged that you need to become more independent at setting up a study schedule for yourself before college, start by reviewing page 89 on setting up a master calendar.

Once your master calendar is complete, use these tips to get the most out of it for studying.

✔ **Count the hours available each day.** Look at where you have some unstructured time in your life.

✔ **Fill those hours.** Think about what activities or tasks might best fit in the open blocks of time. For example: Are there study halls during the day? If so, which tasks might you use it to do?

✔ **Identify your peak attention hours.** What is your attention like after school, and what types of activities might fit then? What about after dinner or at various times on the weekend? Does saving schoolwork until Sunday night really work for you?

✔ **Frame your goals.** Some teens like identifying a specific time block to consistently do a certain type of task—"I will study French vocabulary every period in study hall." Others like to state their goals more flexibly— "I will spend 30 minutes a day studying French, and do 1 hour of math homework a day."

Completing Daily Homework

If you've been diagnosed with ADHD/LD, tackling daily homework might be extremely challenging. A lot of teens with ADHD/LD do great on tests because they can listen in class and easily absorb the material from the class lecture or discussion; but because of executive functioning challenges, they may have a tough time with all the organizational skills needed to handle homework. Some students who like more challenging, creative assignments may hate doing daily, repetitive homework after they've already learned the specific skill being practiced.

Even though college classes rarely have daily, graded homework, many classes do require daily practice to learn skills that build on each other. Foreign languages classes require a slow building of vocabulary, verb conjugations, and other memorization tasks, and math and science classes require daily practice to learn different calculations and

ACADEMIC SKILLS

formulas. Since you have rated this skill one that needs to be worked on, we think the following suggestions might help you.

✔ **Identify the reasons that doing daily homework is tough for you.** Do your troubles lie in another skill area—like lacking a system to keep track of assignments? Or is the problem an organizational one, like needing a system for keeping work from different classes organized? Or is it a motivational problem? Maybe you can't see the value in doing this more boring practice work.

✔ **Develop a system for organization.** If the problem is organization, take a minute and think about what systems you have tried for keeping organized in different classes. Does having multiple folders for each subject really work for you? Would it work better to just have one folder for storing all assignments that are due for homework? What system do you think would work to get the right materials home? Some students immediately put the books that have to go home in their backpack or on a specific shelf in their locker. Or should you go entirely electronic and scan your homework and save it by emailing it to yourself so you won't lose it?

✔ **Work on motivation.** If the problem is attitude or motivation, talk to friends, siblings, or cousins who are already in college, and ask them about the importance of doing daily work. Then try to come up with a reason that doing daily homework is important to you and write up a pep talk on a note card that you can post somewhere prominent, or program that pep talk as a reminder on your cell phone. Learn how to use self-rewards to increase your motivation for doing work that may really be boring and repetitive. What reinforcing activity can you do once the homework is completed?

✔ **Analyze grades.** Look critically at the effect **not** doing homework has had on your grades to date. Make sure you know how each teacher assigns grades to homework.

✔ **Set up a homework schedule.** Think about the best time of day for you to get daily homework done. Is there time in school during study hall? Would it work out for you to stay after school and do homework where tutoring sessions are held, just in case questions arise? Or would you be motivated to go to the community library or a local coffee shop to do daily homework right after school? Doing homework before coming home can prevent the organizational problems some teens have and can also give a sense of being done with school work once you arrive home. These strategies may serve you well in college.

✔ **Evaluate your plan.** Remember to evaluate your daily homework plan by keeping a log of how many homework assignments you completed, what grades you got, and what effect doing homework has had on your learning in the class and your class grade.

Keeping Track of Due Dates

It can be stressful, in college, to discover that due dates are not predictable and that college professors don't give lots of reminders. Instead, professors often expect students to go to the class website and know when tests and papers are due. It's really tricky to keep all this information in your head. In addition, there are lots of other important dates college students need to know, like the deadline for adding and dropping classes, paying tuition bills, registering for the next semester, requesting learning accommodations, meeting with advisers, selecting a major, studying abroad, applying for scholarships, requesting dorm room assignments, buying tickets to sporting events or to social events . . . the list goes on and on. These important dates may be communicated once, via email, and unless you have a system to keep track of them dates, you might miss out on opportunities.

It is great that you have decided to use the time in high school as an opportunity to create a system that works for you and to develop the thought process to become more independent and responsible. To help you work on these skills now, try some or all of the following suggestions.

✔ **Look at what has worked.** Think about what systems you have tried in the past for keeping track of dates and evaluate which have been helpful and which haven't.

✔ **Ask other students how they keep track of assignments.**

✔ **Consider taking a trip to an office supply store** to look at different planners. Remember to think about your learning style and what might work for you, even if it is unconventional. Would using a cell phone work? How about an online calendar like Google Calendar (free) or a software program like Study Rails (http://www.studyrails.com, a monthly fee) that can send email and text reminders? What about a large wipe-off calendar hanging in your room where you can't miss it? Some students use large whiteboards that they write on, or actually write on mirrors with dry erase markers. Get creative and figure out what will work for you. As one college student we met said, "I am not too embarrassed to write things on my hand until I get to my computer. I always have my hand with me!"

✔ **Use your time wisely.** Could you use study hall as a time to send yourself an email or leave a voicemail with all the assignments from the day or to set up an online calendar with new due dates?

Staying on Top of Reading Assignments

Learning directly from reading is a method you'll need for many college classes. Unlike high school, where readings are discussed in class, college classes frequently touch upon the readings in a more abstract way. Professors may synthesize multiple reading assignments on a topic in a class lecture, but still ask very specific questions about each reading on the exams. We have met many students who told us that the only way they were able to complete assignments in high school was to stay up very late reading and, often, re-reading assignments. Some students tell us that their parents read assignments to them; others admit that they never completed reading assignments in the past. Those tactics aren't likely to work in college.

Managing time to stay on top of reading assignments is an important skill for you to develop in high school. Try some or all of the following suggestions to help develop this skill.

✔ **Include time for reading assignments in your schedule.** As part of setting up a study schedule, look at the available time you have each day and on the weekends and decide which blocks of time would be best for completing reading assignments. When is your attention at its peak?

If you take medication to improve attention span, make sure you're scheduling reading assignments (and all homework) for a time when the medication is working.

✔ **Break big reading assignments into daily goals.** For example, you could break up a 200 page novel that is due in 4 weeks into smaller daily assignments of 10 pages each for 20 days.

✔ **Form a study group.** Would you do better at staying on top of reading assignments if you formed a study group of friends who read together and discuss the readings in small pieces?

✔ **Meet with the teacher** who assigned the readings for advice on how to approach the readings more efficiently and for clarification on what key information from the assignment you should be watching for. Once again, this skill of talking directly with teachers can serve you well in the future at college.

✔ **Consider audio.** If reading is not your strength and you would benefit from having an audio version of an assignment, be sure to check out the resources we listed earlier on page 103 for audio books. Look into technology that provides you with an audio version of a reading assignment. Many of these have built in dictionaries to allow you to look up new terms or vocabulary you find confusing, which can be read aloud by the software! Check out the technologies we mention on page 106 to see if these might make keeping on top of your reading assignments easier.

Writing Papers, Studying for Tests, and Completing Projects in a Timely Manner

Learning how to complete a long-term assignment that is not due for a considerable period of time is one of the most challenging skills you will need to master in college. As we have said before, college professors often determine grades based on only two or three exams that span the entire semester. In some classes, one large project or paper may be the only grade for the class, and it may not be due until the last class meeting. It is not uncommon for there to be very little, if

ACADEMIC SKILLS

any discussion, of these long-term assignments as the class meets. The assumption is that the students are staying on top of things.

If you tend to have difficulty breaking a task into parts and get overwhelmed by long term projects, high school is a good time to learn how to handle these. You'll want to learn to define a step-by-step sequence for projects and complete big tasks in increments. Many teens who struggle with ADHD/LD tell us that they often do their best work as a deadline approaches; however, the sheer size of these types of assignments makes it hard to succeed in college with this approach.

Try some or all of these suggestions to complete any long-term assignments you have now, or set some long-terms goals that you can use to practice breaking projects down and completing them in a timely manner.

Many parents have been the reason that teens with ADHD/LD have been successful at getting larger tasks done. They may have acted as parent directors or repairmen and haven't given you space to learn how to do this type of thinking on your own. Is this the case for you? If so, decide now that this is something that you want to do on your own and have a talk with your parents about your decision and the reasoning behind it. Encourage them to collaborate with you so you learn to do the thinking that they have been doing to make sure you complete big assignments and projects.

✔ **Practice.** Consider asking your teachers at school to create some assignments that are not due until late in the semester and to avoid assigning you smaller deadlines along the way. If teachers are willing, it could be helpful to talk about ways to plan for and work on such large tasks with other students.

ACADEMIC SKILLS

✔ **Discuss strategies with an expert.** Talk to the appropriate resource people at school and discuss strategies for handling these types of assignments.

✔ **Create an assignment calendar.** Most approaches to handling big assignments encourage working backwards from a due date. Try creating a semester-long or monthly calendar that may fit on one page, or purchase project planning calendars that are available at office supply stores. At the start of the semester, you can put all important tests and larger assignments on this calendar and create shorter-term due dates for part of the assignment.

✔ **Divide and conquer.** Another approach to long-term assignments is to take a small step each week. Perhaps you can then set aside a specific number of hours each week to work on this project in addition to daily homework. Some teens with ADHD/LD tell us they prefer not to pin down a specific time or day, but would rather have the freedom to know that before the week is over, they need to take a specific step toward completing a project or paper.

✔ **Look for a partner.** Maybe you would like to partner with a friend and then be accountable to each other for completing the smaller steps in the long-term project. Commit to sending each other the first draft of a paper by a specific date.

✔ **Make it fun.** Think about how to make doing these small steps more fun. Think about where to do the work—would a coffee shop be a rewarding environment? How about doing a rewarding activity right after completing a step toward a long term project?

ACADEMIC SKILLS

Part III: Go!

By now you've read up on some differences between high school and college, completed the College Readiness Checklist, set **SMART** goals for yourself, and developed an action plan to achieve those goals. You've also learned specific tips for improving skills and skill areas that you identified as needing work, and have started to gather print and web resources to help you in college and during your prep time. You know that you can return to this book and the resources you've discovered as often as you need to as you refine your goals and modify your plans. All these resources will be there while you practice developing your college readiness skills in high school, and also when you have to put those skills to work on campus. You've begun to stretch and grow, and you've taken concrete steps to make sure you are one of the many students with ADHD/LD who succeed in college, on your own.

Now it's the summer before you take off for college—time to get everything in place. Here are a few more last-minute hints, some words of inspiration, and some more resources for your journey.

PREPARING TO START COLLEGE

Line Up All the Resources You Will Need

Register with the Disability Services office as soon as possible, preferably right after you get your acceptance letter. By now you may already know the person in charge of accepting documentation—if not, call or email the disabilities office to find out who that person is, and submit all of your paperwork as soon as you can. It's important to ask if you will need more testing or additional records from your high school. The ideal situation is for you to start off in your new setting familiar with the people and procedures for arranging everything you need, and with all of your accommodations and services already in place. Be sure to ask about any additional resources that are available on campus for all students. Are there tutoring programs to review course content or workshops on study skills? How about a writing center, a learning center, or a counseling center? If you take medication, how does the student health service handle providing prescriptions?

Also, ask about and sign up for any special programs to help first-year students with and without disabilities transition to college. If none exist, find out if you can take a summer school class before starting college in the fall to mimic a summer transition program.

Implement Any Orientation or Transition Experiences You Have Set Up

Now is the time to implement any of the special transition experiences you learned about to help with your adjustment to college. If you have been accepted into a summer transition program or will be taking a summer school course, begin to use the campus resources during this time so that you will be familiar with everything before classes start in the fall. If you are participating in freshman orientation activities, use the experience to its fullest. Be sure to attend any orientation activities but, between sessions, set up meetings with the campus supports you intend to use so you'll be all set to go on the first day of classes. Find

PART III

out what the schedule is for orientation activities after classes start, if they continue past the first day.

Select a Balanced First-Semester Schedule of Classes

Be sure to disclose your disabilities to your academic advisor, who will help you to choose a fall semester schedule. Even if you submitted documentation to the Disability Services Office, these records are not shared, so unless you disclose your disabilities, most advisors will encourage you to take a typical first semester schedule rather than tailoring a program to fit your specific needs. Now is a good time to start thinking about career exploration activities and choosing a major or area of study, but there is no immediate pressure to declare a major. Also, be sure that you are familiar with the policies for remaining in good standing at the end of the first semester. If there is a system of probation, find out how it works. Be sure to enter the deadlines for adding and dropping classes into your calendar, or set up a reminder system for yourself. Here are some tips for setting up a balanced schedule:

✔ Consider registering for an extra class and have a plan for dropping one.

✔ If you plan to drop a class and take the fewest possible hours you can while still being considered a full-time student, find out if you will need to attend summer school to make up the credits you dropped.

✔ Take a balanced schedule: not too many classes matched to your weaknesses and some that match your strengths.

✔ Try to spread out classes during the day so there are pockets of time to study, prepare for the next class, and schedule testing accommodations.

✔ Pay careful attention to deadlines for adding and dropping classes. Just because you scheduled for a group of classes doesn't mean you have to stick with it if a class doesn't seem right. Once these deadlines pass, though, it is very difficult, if not impossible, to make changes without special circumstances or permission.

PART III

Check Out All the Opportunities
for You to Get Involved on Campus

Feeling connected with others and like you're a part of campus life can be a great way to be reassured that your adjustment to college is on track. Every campus is chock full of student organizations, cultural activities, and opportunities for you to meet other people, improve your talents, foster your passions, and find new interests. Check out the new-student website as well as the campus website to see what is available, and attend any activity fairs that your school sponsors. Ask about any activities that your dorm may be hosting to help new students meet one another and get involved on campus.

It's important to get involved, but you should also think critically about how involved. Being successful academically should be your main goal during your first semester, because the grades you get are critical to your being able to remain in college.

If you are thinking of pledging a fraternity or sorority, find out long before you make this decision what the pledging requirements are. Many students we know found out the hard way that pledging in their first semester was a mistake. Pledging usually involves lots of mandatory meetings and memorizing information and happens during the first few weeks of classes when you might also be dealing with a lot of academic adjustments. You know best what you need, just make sure that you make wise choices. If you are a bit slow to adjust to new places and make friends, finding a niche where you will feel comfortable may be the key to feeling at home. If you love change and meeting new people, but need time to study, prioritize your top interests, think about what you will really have time to do, and choose activities accordingly. Remember—you don't have to do it all in your first semester.

Figure Out Who Does What

Take some time reviewing the college website (and involve your parents) and find out how the offices on your campus are organized and where they are located. Don't be afraid to ask for help; often the office that is responsible for new student activities can provide guidance to any student who needs it—that's what they are there for. Campus can be a confusing place, especially if you are used to everything being in one building. The following are some of the common questions that we find new students frequently have:

- Where do I get my student ID? Does my ID card act as my bank card?

- How and where do I get my meals?

- How do I change my schedule and what are the deadlines?

- Where do I go if I have questions about my dorm and housing?

- How do I register my car, bike, motorcycle, or scooter?

- What is the campus bus schedule?

- Which library do I use?

- Where will I do my laundry?

- How do I know what my vacation schedule is?

- If I live out of state, how do I get to and from the airport?

- If I am on financial aid, where is that office and how do I get my aid?

- How do I get tickets to sporting events?

- What do I do if I am sick?

- What help is there for me if I am really homesick or having trouble adjusting?

Once you get your fall schedule, it might also help to walk the campus while your parents are still around to find the buildings where your classes are held and to see how long it really takes to get from your dorm to your first class and from one class to another.

The more you know about your new world at college, the more comfortable you will feel when you are on your own.

PART III

A FEW FINAL WORDS

We know that this guide is asking you to do a lot of hard work. If you need inspiration, check out what it will take for you to get accepted at the college of your dreams. Consider visiting a campus and talking to college students with disabilities like yours and ask them what they wished they had done during high school.

Here's what one college student with ADHD and LD said when we asked her what advice she would give to high school students about how to succeed in college:

"Find inspiration! And renew it regularly. Make sure you seek out people who have ADHD/LD who are inspiring and leading successful lives. Whether it is a famous person or a local mentor or friend, you need someone to look up to. It is important to know that ADHD/LD isn't some terrible disease, but that it is a difference and that there are two sides to every coin. On one side, this difference can make it harder for you to learn and do things, but the other gives you special talents and allows you to see things from a different perspective. Believe in yourself and find your own ways to develop your skills."

Remember and believe...
you can be successful in college!

REFERENCES

Barkley, R. A., Murphy, K. R., & Fischer, M. (2007). Adults with ADHD: Clinic-referred cases vs. children grown up. *ADHD Report,* 15(5), 1–7, 13.

D'Amico, Aurora. Email: January 29, 2008.

Heiligenstein, E., Guenther, G., Levey, A., Savino, F., & Fulwiler, J. (1999). Psychological and academic functioning in college students with attention deficit hyperactivity disorder. *Journal of American College Health,* 47, 181–185.

Kadison, R., & DiGeronimo, T. F. (2004). *College of the overwhelmed: The campus mental health crisis and what to do about it.* San Francisco, CA: Jossey-Bass.

Klein, A. *Incoming college students rate emotional health at record low, annual survey finds.* Retrieved Feb. 2, 2011 from **http://newsroom.ucla.edu/portal/ucla/incoming-college-students-self-191135.aspx.**

Murray, C., Goldstein, D., Nourse, S., & Edgar, E. (2000). The postsecondary school attendance and completion rates of high school graduates with LD. *Learning Disabilities Research and Practice,* 15, 119–127.

National Center for Education Statistics. (2000). *Postsecondary students with disabilities: Enrollment, services and persistence* (NCES 2000–092). Washington, DC: U.S. Department of Education. Retrieved from **http://nces.ed.gov/pubs2000/2000092.pdf**

National Center for Education Statistics. (2002). *Descriptive summary of 1995–96 beginning postsecondary students: Six years later* (NCES 2003-151). Washington, DC: U.S. Department of Education. Retrieved from **http://nces.ed.gov/pubsearch/pubsinfo.asp?pubid=2003151** National Center for Education Statistics. (2003).

Newman, L., Wagner, M., Cameto, R., & Knokey, A. M. (2009). *The post-high school outcomes of youth with disabilities up to 4 years after high school: A report from the National Longitudinal Transition Study–2* (NLTS2) (NCSER 2009-3017). Retrieved from **www.nlts2.Org/reports/2009_04/nlts2_report_2009_04_complete.pdf**

Rabiner, D., Anastopoulos, A., Costello, J., Hoyle, R., & Swartzwelder, H. (2008). Adjustment to college in students with ADHD. *Journal of Attention Disorders, 11,* 689–699.

Sieben, L. College freshmen report record low levels of emotional health. *The Chronicle of Higher Education.* January 27, 2011. Retrieved from **http://www.gao .gov/new.items/d1033.pdf**

Vogel, S., & Adelman, P. (1990a). Extrinsic and intrinsic factors in graduation and academic failure among LD college students. *Annals of Dyslexia (Orton Dyslexia Society),* 40, 119–137.

Vogel, S., & Adelman, P. (1990b). Intervention effectiveness at the postsecondary level for the learning disabled. In T. Scruggs & B. Wong (Eds.), *Intervention research in learning disabilities* (pp. 329–344). New York, NY: Springer-Verlag.

Vogel, S., & Adelman, P. (2000). Adults with learning disabilities 8–15 years after college. *Learning Disabilities: A Multidisciplinary Journal,* 10, 165–182.

Vogel, S., Leonard, F., Scales, W., Hayeslip, P., Hermansen, J., & Donnells, L. (1998). The national learning disabilities postsecondary data bank: An overview. *Journal of Learning Disabilities,* 31, 234–247.

Vogel, S., Leyser, Y., Wyland, S., & Brulle, A. (1999). Students with learning disabilities in higher education: Faculty attitudes and practices. *Learning Disabilities Research & Practice,* 14, 173–186.